The World of a Beehive

other titles in the series

THE WORLD OF A
BEEHIVE

John Powell
B.Sc., Master Beekeeper

with line drawings by Wilhelmina Mary Guymer

FABER AND FABER
London · Boston

First published in 1979
by Faber and Faber Limited
3 Queen Square London WC1
Printed in Great Britain by
BAS Printers Limited
Over Wallop Hampshire
All rights reserved

British Library Cataloguing in Publication Data

Powell, John
  World of a beehive.
  1. Bees—Juvenile literature
  I. Title
  595.7'99   QL568.A6
  ISBN 0-571-11341-9

Contents

Illustrations

Plates

(All photographs, with the exception of Plate 25, are by the author)

Figures

Acknowledgements

I am very grateful to Wilhelmina Mary Guymer for her splendid line drawings. Some of these have been put together with great skill from photomicrographs.

I thank Peter Foote, B.Sc., for many helpful comments and suggestions during the preparation of the text and Diana Keetes for typing the complete manuscript and helping me check it.

My thanks are also due to my young friends Josephine English, who posed for one of the photographs, and Jane Archer, for reading through the completed text.

Foreword

Most people find the honeybee fascinating. Perhaps it is the similarity between the bees' communal life and our civilizations, or their ordered society based on the industry of its citizens, that commands our attention. Perhaps it is the dark secrecy of their home, their precious golden stores so well guarded, or their mysterious language. Whatever it may be, here is a creature on which we depend for much of our food. To study it, at first hand, is the privilege of the beekeeper, for he alone can enter into its world, a world vastly different from ours, a world built upon an intimate relationship between plants and insects.

There are many technical terms which I need to use and which you are sure to find in other books. To draw your attention to them, they are printed in italics the first time they appear in the text.

1 · The Community of the Bees

Throughout the animal kingdom, species that live in groups—packs, flocks or shoals—are commonplace. In almost all cases the advantage is that the individuals are safer. Otherwise there is usually little or no co-operation between them; each leads its own existence within the loose framework of the group. Much higher degrees of co-operation can be observed within the unit we would call the family. For instance, parent birds share the work of nest-building, incubating and rearing the young, even providing food for each other. This behaviour can be seen in a highly developed state in ourselves. We depend upon each other to such a great extent that it is virtually impossible for man to live an isolated existence. We live in a complex *society*.

Various degrees of co-operation can be found in the insect world and this book is concerned with the most complex of insect societies—the honeybee (*Apis mellifera*). In order to understand just what is so special about the honeybees' way of life we need first to examine their place in the insect kingdom.

Social insects

The majority of the half-million or so known insect species live solitary lives. Some, like the locust (*Schistocerca gregaria*), obtain protection from predators by living together in groups, while others come together in swarms for mating. An example is the common gnat (*Culex pipiens*).

There are, however, some who live together in colonies, sharing the work of building their nest and providing food. These are the *social insects*—ants, termites, wasps, hornets and bees. Their colonies may vary in size from as few as fifty individuals in the case of some bumblebees to many thousands in the case of ants, termites and honeybees. However, in many cases the colonies do not last all through the year. The colonies are *annual* and are only to be found from spring to autumn. It is only the fertile females or *queens* that are able to hibernate through the winter months. In spring each queen begins the laborious task of establishing her nest and finding food for her young. On mild days in March you have probably noticed large queen bumblebees (*Bombus sp.*), searching for nesting sites on sheltered banks and in hedge-bottoms.

At first each queen lays only a few eggs and these follow the usual course of insect development, hatching into *larvae* which when fully grown begin the amazing process of transformation into the adult insect or *imago*. This process is called *pupation* or *metamorphosis* and the young at this stage, a *pupa*. Before pupation, the larvae spin a cocoon of a fine silken thread as a protection. The changes the insect goes through are so dramatic that it is difficult to believe that the imago really could have begun life as the larva, but no doubt you are familiar with the development of the butterfly from the egg (ovum) through caterpillar (larva) and chrysalis (pupa) to butterfly (imago).

It is only during the larval stage that the insect actually grows. In the case of many social insects, food for their growth has to be collected by the mother queen. The larvae of many species are provided with all the food they need before they hatch from the egg (we call this *mass provisioned*), while other species like the wasps feed their larvae regularly as they grow (*batch provisioned*). Life for the queen during these early days is spent constantly foraging for food.

Eventually the first of her young attain adulthood. Often they are diminutive when compared to their mother, for their growth has been stunted through insufficient food. Nevertheless they are capable of tending the larvae and of foraging. Although they are female their bodily development has not been complete, so that they are not able to mate and lay eggs. Their role in life is to assist the queen in rearing subsequent batches of *brood*, the term we apply collectively to all the juvenile forms, eggs, larvae and pupae. These undeveloped females are called *workers*. As the season progresses the brood is better cared for, as an increasing number of workers share the task. Eventually the queen is able to devote all her time to laying eggs and the colony increases rapidly. At last fully developed females (queens) are produced and males are reared. The climax of the season occurs when the newly reared queens leave their home in search of a mate. Shortly after fertilization these queens seek out suitable places for hibernation. The workers, males and old queen die with the onset of autumn. So the process is able to repeat itself year after year.

Bees

Within the groups of insects we call bees we find both non-social solitary bees like the mining bees (*Adrena amata*) and the leaf-cutter bees (*Megachile sp.*) and also social bees like the genus *Bombus*, the bumblebees. Bumblebees have annual colonies. The social bees of the genus *Apis*, the honeybee, have advanced still further in their social behaviour. They differ from other social bees in that they do not hibernate. Instead they store food to tide them over the winter period so that the colony can maintain itself from one season to the next. Their colonies are *perennial*.

Honeybees

There are four species of honeybee, *Apis florea*, the little honeybee; *Apis dorsata*, the giant honeybee; *Apis cerana*, the eastern honeybee; and *Apis mellifera*, the western honeybee. The little and giant honeybees live in relatively small colonies of up to a few hundred workers. They are essentially tropical insects, living in southern Asia. *Apis cerana*, the eastern honeybee, is a sub-tropical insect and has larger colonies, which frequently attain 15,000 workers. Its habitat is the Indian sub-continent, where it is of some economic importance as a honey producer. The western honeybee lives in large colonies with a complicated social organization. It ranges naturally from North Africa and the Mediterranean shores, northwards throughout

Europe and eastwards into Russia and Turkey. It has been much exploited by man and taken to temperate regions throughout the world—to Canada, the U.S.A., South America, Australia and New Zealand. It is the honeybee which we find working in our gardens and which has been associated with European and African civilizations for nine thousand years or more. From now onwards we shall concentrate our attention on this creature and refer to it simply as the 'bee' or the 'honeybee'.

The honeybee

A colony of honeybees contains three distinct kinds or *castes* of adult bees—the queen, the worker and the *drone* or male bee—together with its brood. Each caste has its own unique functions to fulfil and has evolved to a point of extreme specialization.

(a) THE QUEEN

Each colony has one queen and she is the mother of her workers and drones. Like the queens of other social insects, she alone can be fertilized and lay eggs. However, the queen honeybee can no longer build her own nest and is quite unable to forage for food; indeed, she

Plate 1 The queen honeybee (*Apis mellifera*) spends all her life egglaying. This queen has been marked on her thorax. Note the behaviour of the workers round about her.

does not even feed herself. Instead, all the functions needed to construct and maintain the colony have been taken over by the workers. Free from all other tasks, the queen devotes her life to laying eggs, and her body has become supremely adapted to this function. During the spring a honeybee queen can lay as many as two thousand eggs in a single day, although half this number is perhaps more usual. This is considerably in excess of her own body weight and represents an average of nearly one egg every minute. She is constantly being fed by the workers, who regulate her rate of egg production by the amount of food they offer her. In exchange they lick from her body a secretion for which they crave. This is a complex chemical *pheromone* called 'queen substance'.

(b) THE WORKERS

The workers, like the workers of other social insects, are female. They are, however, incapable of mating; in very exceptional circumstances they are able to lay a few eggs, but normally their ovaries are kept inactive by the presence of queen substance. Worker honeybees are highly specialized creatures and carry on their bodies all the 'tools' they need to cope with the varied tasks they undertake, even producing the material from which the nest is built—*beeswax*. In contrast to the workers of annual colonies, worker honeybees are always present, summer and winter alike. They are the most numerous of the three castes. A large colony in summer may have as many as 60,000.

(c) THE DRONES

Drones are the male bees, and are present only during the times of prosperity, spring and summer. As autumn approaches they are banished from the colony by the workers and left to die. It must be said that, as yet, we understand very little about the function they serve within the community. It is true that they spend a lot of their time within the hive and that they are seldom observed feeding themselves, preferring to be fed by their sisters. They take flights only on warm days, and it is easy to picture them as lazy, good-for-nothing creatures. Yet if we deliberately deprive a colony of its

Fig. 1 The three castes of the honeybee—the female queen and worker, and the male drone.

drones, that colony seems to lose its drive to work and becomes demoralized. It is during flight that the drone seeks to fulfil his primary function of fertilizing a young queen. Few succeed, for each colony will raise more drones than could possibly be needed. Quite often, several thousand have been raised by high summer. In common with many insect species the honeybee male dies in the mating act.

With this outline picture of the honeybee colony, one mother queen with her daughters (workers) and sons (drones), we are in a position to take a detailed look at their complex civilization.

The nest

The nest of the honeybee is superbly engineered from the point of view both of strength and of efficient use of space and material. It provides accommodation for the brood, space for the storage of food supplies and a permanent home for the adults. It is fashioned entirely from beeswax—a product of the bees' own bodies. The nest is usually built within a dark, weatherproof cavity, although occasionally bees will build in the open. Hollow trees and small caves are popular places in the wild, but man has unwittingly provided many suitable localities: lofts, chimneys, sheds, barns, church spires, even derelict

Fig. 2 The nest of a bumblebee (*Bombus lucorum*). Note the haphazard arrangement of the cells.

Plate 2 The honeybee seldom builds its combs in the open. This colony would not have survived the winter in this exposed position.

motor cars. Once a suitable location has been found the bees begin by depositing wax on the uppermost support and proceed to extend their *combs* downwards from this. At intervals the combs are braced together and to side supports for strength. It is the pattern to which bees construct the comb itself that has captured man's imagination from early times. There is usually no shortage of space for the small colonies of the bumblebees, and they construct an haphazard arrangement of barrel-shaped wax cells in which to rear their brood. The honeybee has adapted cylindrical cells to her own use, packing them together in an ordered array to make most efficient use of both space and beeswax.

(a) COMB CONSTRUCTION

Try making some small paper rings of equal size and fit as many as you can within a frame. If you fill the frame without distorting the rings you will find there will be waste space between them. Now try to fit in more by distorting the rings. Triangles fit together well, but the space within would be unsuitable for a bee larva; squares are better, but the most effective shape is the hexagon—the shape the bees use. Not only do they construct their combs from close-packed hexagonal cells, they arrange for the bases of the cells to form a vertical wall so that they can be fitted together back-to-back. The base of each cell fits neatly with two of its neighbours on the opposite side of the mid-rib of the comb. Also the axis of each cell is given a slight upward tilt towards the mouth so that liquids do not run out. This construction is immensely strong; 50 grammes of beeswax is easily able to support 2 kilogrammes of honey. Figure 3 illustrates the construction of comb.

(b) PROPOLIS

One other material is used by bees for construction, a resinous substance called *propolis*. This is gathered by the workers from the buds and bark of trees and shrubs. It is soft and sticky (like toffee) when collected but hardens with time and in cold weather becomes brittle. Bees use it to waterproof their home, for filling in small cracks and cavities and for restricting the size of the entrance to keep out enemies. Besides being waterproof, propolis has some unusual

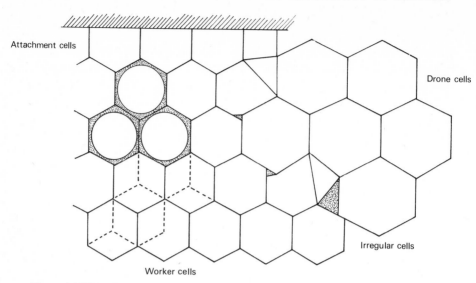

Fig. 3 (a) This diagram shows the geometric construction of comb. The cells on the other side of the mid-rib are shown dotted. Where worker cells merge with drone cells, irregularly shaped cells are built. The hexagonal shape is modified also where comb is attached to a support. You can also see how the bees shape the mouths of the cells into a circle.

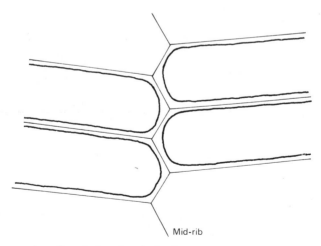

(b) A cross-section of comb showing the back to back arrangement of the cells and the slight upward tilt towards the mouth.

properties and is thought to contain an antibiotic agent. It is the subject of much research at the present time, for it clearly plays an important part in the hygiene of the nest. Bees carry away small items of debris, but the larger items they cannot move are coated with propolis. I once found a perfectly preserved mouse inside a hive. The bees, being unable to remove the body, had embalmed it with propolis.

(c) THE BEE-SPACE

It is remarkable how bees can build comb with great precision, usually in complete darkness. One point we should emphasize here is their use of space within their home. The combs are built at a uniform

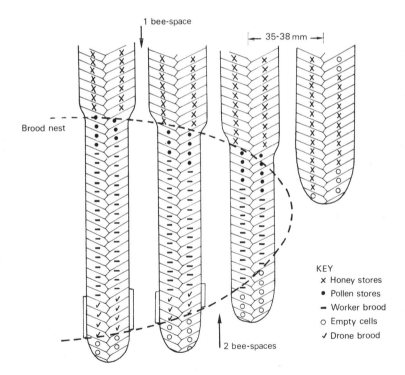

Fig. 4 The arrangement of the nest. Use this diagram in conjunction with Plates 2 and 8.

distance from each other, leaving just sufficient space between to allow the bees to work on adjacent faces. Somehow they manage to gauge this distance accurately as they commence building, so as to leave a passageway of 6 to 8 millimetres between the faces. This means that the mid-ribs need to be spaced between 35 and 38 millimetres apart. These passageways are known as *bee-spaces*. Bee-spaces are of great importance in the design of the modern hive. Any gap larger than a bee-space is eventually filled with more comb; any smaller gap is sealed with propolis. Figure 4 illustrates the arrangement of the nest and the spacing of the combs.

Bees may build combs which are entirely worker cells or drone cells, but more frequently they build a mixture of both. Since drone cells are slightly larger than worker cells the regularity of the pattern is spoilt when one kind of comb gives way to the other, as Figure 3 shows.

The food of the bees

(a) HONEY

The combs provide the bees with accommodation for rearing the brood and storage space for reserves of food. They need to store food because the colony is perennial. Since the queen does not pass the winter in hibernation—that is, in a state where her body temperature is allowed to fall to that of the surroundings—warmth is needed to maintain activity throughout the cold winter months. We shall see later that honey contains sugars, and it is the digestion of these sugars within the worker-bees' bodies which provides them with heat. Honey is prepared from the nectar of flowers during the warmer months and preserved in cells of the comb—honeycomb—for use in the winter. Honey provides the carbohydrate food for the bees, giving energy to their muscles and heat to their bodies. It may seem strange to find that insects are warm-bodied, but when large numbers are massed together, as in a honeybee colony, they produce a good deal of heat. This heat is used to incubate the brood in the active season and to keep out the cold in the winter.

(b) POLLEN

All creatures need not only carbohydrate food but also protein. Protein is the part of the diet which permits growth—the 'building bricks' of the body. All kinds of bees are truly vegetarian and obtain their protein from the pollen of flowers, unlike wasps, which are carnivorous. Honeybees are able to store pollen in the combs for use early in the season before there are many flowers available, and are therefore able to rear brood and build up their population at a time when most hibernating species have scarcely begun their nests. This characteristic is of immense value to man for the pollination of early-flowering crops. Cells in which honey and pollen are stored are closed with a wax capping across the mouth to protect the contents from moisture.

(c) WATER

Water is not strictly a food, yet it is vitally necessary to life. One of the first activities we observe our bees doing in spring is collecting water. This they do from the warm, sunny edges of streams and ponds, from water-logged soil, even from cow-pats and the drain from the kitchen sink. Bees need water whenever brood-rearing is taking place, in order to dilute honey and to maintain the humidity within the nest.

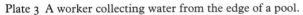

Plate 3 A worker collecting water from the edge of a pool.

Water is collected and carried in the same way as nectar. You will find
this described in Chapter 4. Once this activity has begun it is
continued in all but the most severe weather. Water-carriers become
easily chilled and thereby unable to fly; some are dashed by the wind
against the water surface and are drowned. Water-collecting is a risky
business and early in the year many bees may lose their lives in this
activity.

Throughout the season the collection of water continues unabated
except for the occasions when large amounts of nectar are being
brought in. Then the bees may have too much and the labour of
collection is changed to the labour of ventilation as they evaporate the
excess. Standing in an orderly formation, they drive a current of
warm, moist air from the entrance of their home by fanning with their
wings. In very hot weather bees collect water and evaporate it within
the confines of the combs as a deliberate means for cooling the hive.
The combined effect of the heat from their bodies, ventilation by
fanning and the cooling produced by the evaporation of water enables
the bees to obtain the precise temperature control needed for the
proper incubation of the brood. This temperature is roughly the same
as our bodies and lies between 35 and 37°C.

The colony throughout the year

Let us now look briefly at the colony as it develops throughout the
year. For convenience we will begin during the winter period, when
activity is at its lowest ebb.

(a) WINTER

Winter is a quiet period for the honeybee colony. Provided it has been
successful during the active season it will have adequate supplies of
honey and pollen stored within its combs to tide it over until the
spring. The colony at this season consists of the queen and
approximately 10,000 to 20,000 workers but no drones. Winter starts
(in Britain) with the first frosts from early October onwards and lasts
until the early spring flowers present their pollen, maybe from late in
January or during February. Of course, these dates vary considerably

with the weather. During this time the bees of the colony remain clustered together on the combs, generating heat to keep themselves warm by consuming the honey stores. The cluster first forms towards the lower parts of the combs and gradually moves upwards as the stores are used. As the bees open the cappings to reach their larder, particles of wax are discarded and fall to the floor. The general upward movement avoids contamination of unused stores. Healthy bees void their excreta in flight, away from their hive. Their rectum is capable of considerable distension to accommodate waste matter for long periods. On mild days in winter bees may be observed taking cleansing flights. These mild spells give the bees an opportunity to break cluster and re-form on another portion of the combs, thereby gaining access to fresh stores. Occasionally, in prolonged severe weather, a colony may starve to death simply because the cluster has not had this opportunity to reach other parts of its stores. The winter cluster typically may consume 7 to 10 kilogrammes of honey.

Although the bees keep warm, they do not regulate the temperature exactly or attempt to remove excess moisture by ventilation. Temperature regulation is achieved by varying the density of the cluster—in cold spells the bees cluster tightly together, in milder times they cluster more loosely. The queen lays very few eggs during this period, so that frequently no brood is present at all.

(b) SPRING

As the new year advances and the days lengthen, the early spring flowers respond by presenting their pollen and nectar. In favourable weather the foragers will set out in search of these and the water-gatherers will be out too. Now the pattern of life within the colony changes. The temperature in the centre of the combs is raised. Cells are cleaned in preparation, and in response to the arrival of fresh pollen the queen begins her mammoth task of restoring the population to its summer level. At first only a few eggs are laid each day, but as these bees become of age the rate increases rapidly. The demand for food, both honey (or nectar) and pollen increases also. The colony can draw on the remains of its stored reserves, but the need for fresh supplies becomes ever more urgent. The rate at which expansion can take place depends on the food reserves and available supplies. A colony may use as much food in three or four weeks in March as it had previously used all winter! If the spring is cool and wet, starvation is an ever-present threat.

Brood-rearing is well under way by mid-March and reaches its peak late in April. By this time more than 1,000 bees may be born each day. At some stage in the spring, when the population is predominantly young bees of the current year, drones are reared— the colony is preparing for summer.

(c) SUMMER

For the honeybee colony, summer is the focus of the year, though the bees' summer comes earlier than ours. It includes the period of the major honey-producing crops, the fruit blossoms, white clover (*Trifolium repens*) and the limes (*Tilia sp.*) and encompasses the months of May, June and July. The peak development of the colony has been reached and during this period actually begins to diminish. The collection and processing of nectar are the prime activities for much of this time, but for many colonies another comes into prominence—*swarming*.

Social animals like the bees, wasps or ants need to reproduce at two levels—firstly they need to reproduce the individuals that make up the colony and secondly they need to replenish the colonies which have met with misfortune. The annual social insects rear a number of queens and these, after mating, found independent colonies. The situation is somewhat different with those perennial social insects where the queens are no longer able to fend for themselves. Instead a method has been evolved whereby the colony divides. During the summer period of prosperity a colony will prepare to rear queens. I will describe later how this can be done (see p. 43). When the first of these queen larvae has been sealed into its cell ready to pupate, the existing queen will leave with a swarm. From noon until mid-afternoon is the usual time, but a swarm may be delayed by bad weather. Up to a third of the worker population will pour out of the hive and take to the air in a milling throng. The queen will join them and take wing. Slowly the new swarm will move away from the parent

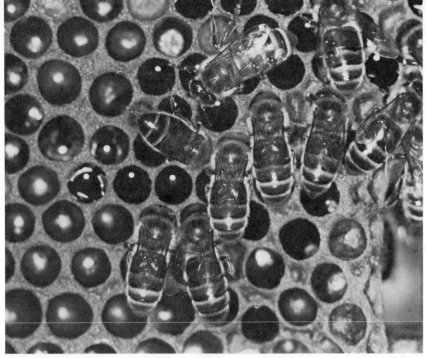

Plate 4 Workers gorging on honey prior to the departure of a swarm. Smoke also causes bees to gorge, making them less inclined to sting.

colony, the bees zig-zagging through the flying mass to maintain contact.

A swarm seldom travels far to begin with, maybe 50 to 100 metres, and then settles to form a dense cluster. Normally a branch of a tree is chosen within 5 metres of the ground, allowing the cluster to hang freely. With the excitement of the initial swarm over, the bees wait quietly while a new home is found. For some days before, scout-bees will have been searching for a likely home and will now renew their activity. Eventually they will be able to communicate their choice to the rest of the swarm, which will again take to the air. Once reclustered in their new home, be it a hollow tree or a chimney, the bees will set about the task of elaborating wax and building comb. The queen will begin laying, the foragers will work with increased vigour on the late summer crops and the new unit will be well established before winter begins.

But what about the parent colony? As they no longer have a queen,

Plate 5 A swarm hanging in a bush. There were about 10,000 bees in this cluster.

no further egg-laying can take place, but the existing brood continues to mature, partially replacing the adults lost with the swarm. A week after the swarm has left, the first of the new queens will be ready to emerge from her cell and within the next few days so will her sisters. As each princess emerges, she leaves the nest with a *cast*—a miniature swarm—of a few hundred bees until the colony has become so depleted that no more queens are needed and remaining queen cells are destroyed.

The last princess to be born is retained by the parent colony. This unit has the advantage of possessing the combs and stores of the original nest. Whereas few drones accompany the swarm, there will be many in each of the casts. A cast clusters like a swarm while its scouts find it a home. Here the bees wait until their queen has been mated, then they set to work to build comb and gather food. As they are a small unit their survival is very much at risk in a poor summer.

So the colony has reproduced itself—a swarm and several casts. Each unit spends the remainder of the summer engaged in increasing its population and storing food in anticipation of winter.

(d) AUTUMN

By the end of July, the summer period of prosperity has passed. Autumn has arrived for the honeybee colony. The drones are ruthlessly removed from the hive, for the colony cannot tolerate unnecessary demands on its winter rations. There are many minor sources of nectar and pollen in August and September and the bees devote themselves to gathering from these. Sometimes a field of late mustard (*Sinapsis alba*) or red clover (*Trifolium pratense*) will provide a major income. The situation is very different where bees have access to the upland moors. Here the ling heather (*Calluna vulgaris*) can provide a large intake in good weather. A limited amount of brood will be reared from these late sources and it is these bees that are so important to the colony for its success the following year. Young bees in autumn eat large amounts of fresh pollen. This is converted to fat and stored by their bodies. These fat reserves help the bees to survive the winter and are broken down to brood-food in the following spring. As the nights become colder, the winter cluster begins to form. The year is complete.

2 · A Life's Work

Let us now look at the lives of the individuals that make up a colony. Since the worker leads by far the most varied and interesting existence we shall study her first.

The worker

For convenience the life span of the worker can be divided into three roughly equal periods, each of three weeks. The first of these is spent confined within the cells of the comb in the juvenile form as brood, the second as an adult within the hive and the third as an adult forager. Whereas the length of the brood stage is fixed, there is a good deal of variation in the adult's life, depending upon the circumstances within the colony. We will concentrate on a typical worker-bee in a mature colony during the summer months.

(a) JUVENILE FORMS

Life begins when an egg is laid by the queen in a worker cell. Just prior to this the cell will have been carefully cleaned by some of the youngest adults. When laid an egg is about 1.5 millimetres long, banana-shaped and an opaque white in colour. It is attached to the base of the cell by one end and points away from the base along the axis of the cell. At the end of 3 days it will have turned so as to lie in contact with the base of the cell and will also have become almost transparent.

As the larva is about to hatch, the first supply of *brood-food* is placed alongside. Brood-food is a secretion of the *hypopharyngeal*

Plate 6 Eggs and larvae. Note the pools of brood-food surrounding the younger larvae.

glands of young adults. It is a whitish fluid with a slightly bitter taste; it is rich in protein, vitamins and minerals, and contains some sugars. Brood-food contains everything the larva needs for growth and like milk in mammals is almost completely digestible, producing little waste matter. The newly emerged larva is no larger than the egg from which it came and lies on one side in its pool of brood-food, moving occasionally to reach a fresh area. Being batch-provisioned, the larva receives regular meals throughout its growth. It is estimated that, on average, feeding takes place at the astonishing frequency of once every minute. The rate of growth is equally amazing. In the 5 days of the larval stage, its weight increases some 1,500 times! At this rate of growth a human baby would weigh about 4.5 tonnes.

As the larva grows it takes 4 short rests from feeding, during which it moults—just like the caterpillars of butterflies and moths. In common with other insects, the bee carries its skeleton on the outside of its body. Because it is outside, this type of skeleton is called an exo-skeleton. It has the advantage of being both very strong and very light, but when fully hardened, as in the adult stage, it restricts the bee's capacity to grow. Growth is only possible, therefore, during the larval stages, when the exo-skeleton is softer and the moults allow the

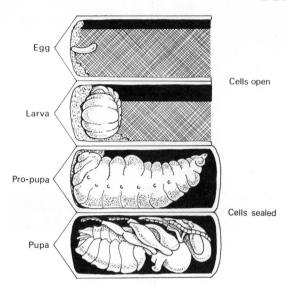

Fig. 5 Juvenile forms of the worker. The drone is reared in a similar way but the queen has her own special downward-facing cell.

creature to dispose of its tight outer skin and replace it with a larger one. The larvae breathe through small ports (*spiracles*) in their sides which connect with a network of tubes (*trachaea*), conveying oxygen into their body tissues and waste carbon dioxide out.

When fully grown the larva practically fills the cell, and is curled like a letter 'C'. At this stage it receives its last meal and is sealed into its cell by the adult workers with a capping of porous wax. This protects the larva during pupation while allowing it to breathe. The fat larva then stretches itself along the axis of the cell, head end outermost, and undergoes its last moult. Shortly afterwards it excretes the accumulated waste products from its rectum and spins a cocoon made of a silk-like thread from glands near its mouthparts. With this activity over the larva—now called a pro-pupa—rests on its back.

For the next twelve days its body undergoes the complete transformation of metamorphosis. The body becomes differentiated into three distinct sections—the *head*, the *thorax* and the *abdomen*. The *eyes*, *antennae* and *proboscis* form on the head, *legs* and *wings* on the thorax, and the internal organs and *sting* in the abdomen. Gradually the body darkens from pearly white through purple and tan to the yellow and brown of the imago. Twenty-one days after the egg was laid pupation is complete. The young bee becomes restless in her cell, her jaws or mandibles pierce through the wax capping of her cell and, aided by adults outside, she laboriously bites her way to freedom and the adult world.

(b) THE YOUNG ADULT

Hitherto she has been static within her cell, now she enters the bustle of the colony. Henceforth her life will be one of constant toil and an ever-changing series of roles. From the moment of her emergence she is fully grown, for her exo-skeleton is fully formed. At first she is downy and rather damp. In the next few hours the hair on her body will dry and harden. The exo-skeleton will harden too. After a short period of rest she will seek food from her older sisters and then join in with the work of the community. At first she will clean cells like the one from which she herself emerged, removing any debris and varnishing the base with saliva, ready for the queen to lay eggs in. From her second day she will visit the pollen stores and eat large

Plate 7 Mature larvae nearly 5 days old and pupating brood beneath the porous wax cappings.

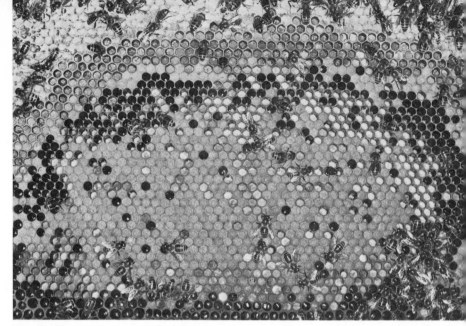

Plate 8 The arrangement of a typical comb. Sealed brood in the centre is surrounded by younger unsealed larvae and eggs. Around these are the pollen stores and, at the top, sealed honey stores.

quantities of pollen. This is digested in the ventriculus, releasing protein which is absorbed into the body fluids as it passes through the intestine. Nourished from the body fluid, the hypopharyngeal glands, situated in the head, develop and shortly begin to produce brood-food.

The young worker now begins to turn her attention to feeding the brood. At first she feeds the oldest larvae and then, as her glands become fully developed, she feeds younger ones. For the next eight or ten days of her life she will be fully occupied as a *nurse-bee*, all day and all night, for activity within the brood nest never ceases. As the hypopharyngeal glands decline so the *wax glands* become active. At this stage in her life the bee may consume large quantities of nectar or honey, which her body converts into beeswax. The young worker now joins with a team of other comb-building bees. These hang in a characteristic loose cluster, supporting each other, linked foot to foot. The clusters generate considerable warmth as, slowly, scales of wax are produced. These are about the size of a pinhead and are passed from bee to bee to the site where comb is being built. It is not surprising that we find large numbers of bees of this age, 10 to 20 days old, in a swarm, for its first task must be to build comb.

At any time during the first fortnight of adult life, a young worker may take short flights. These flights allow the bees to learn the location of their home and become familiar with the surroundings. They often take place at one specific time of the day and beekeepers refer to them as 'play-flights'. Towards the end of the bees' period as comb-builders, as the wax glands decline, play-flights are made more frequently and become longer. The bee first learns the appearance

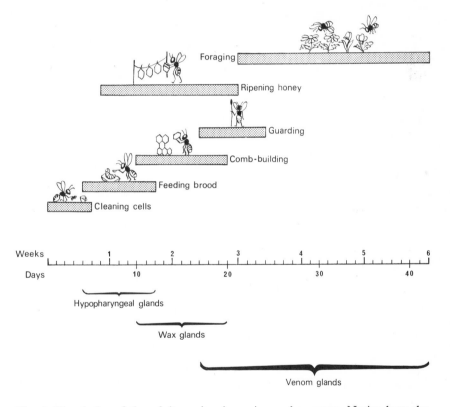

Fig. 6 The duties of the adult worker in spring and summer. Notice how the progression of tasks overlap and are related to the development of three important glands.

and smell of the entrance and then the surroundings, flying in ever larger circles around the hive. Between play-flights, many do duty as *guard-bees*, inspecting all who enter the nest, and repelling intruders. The venom glands of the sting will have become fully developed by now. Not all bees become either comb-builders or guard-bees, and some may undertake these activities for a short while only. Instead they will be employed as *house-bees*, engaged particularly in ripening nectar into honey and in the storage of pollen.

All the duties I have described tend to merge together and overlap. Together they cover the internal needs of the colony and the chart on page 41 illustrates this second phase in the workers' life. As you can see, these activities follow an ordered sequence based on the development of the various glands. Nevertheless, no bee ever completely loses its ability to perform any function; ultimately it is the need of the colony that overrides all other factors.

(c) THE FORAGER

Sooner or later, the play-flights turn into foraging flights. From now until her death, the worker spends as much time in the fields as the flora and weather allow. Pollen and nectar are gathered as the need arises, often both together. The collection of either water or of propolis tend to be regarded as 'specialist' jobs, being left to a relatively few individuals, and it would appear that a small minority become engaged as scout-bees, whose specific task is to locate crops or to search for a new home for a swarm. Foraging is an exhausting as well as a dangerous business. Muscle fibres become worn out and weaken with age. The wings on which all this activity depends become torn and frayed. Sooner or later the forager is unable to become airborne and she perishes, usually away from home, just 9 short weeks after she first began as an egg.

(d) WINTER BEES

Bees born in the autumn are not required to act as nurse-bees or wax-builders or even to do much foraging until the following spring. Instead, the pollen they eat early in life provides their bodies with a layer of fat to act as a protein reserve to enable them to endure the winter. Theirs is a long, but dull life until spring comes. Then the feverish activity quickly wears them out. Even so, bees born in August will frequently live until well into the following April.

The queen

By comparison with the worker, the queen leads a very dull existence. The name 'queen' is perhaps misleading, implying, as it does, some kind of regal or ruling function. Nothing could be further from the truth, for all the 'decisions' made by the colony are taken by the collective and instinctive behaviour of the workers. However, the life of the colony centres on the queen, since she alone provides for the continuity of life within it. She has a considerably longer life span than her workers, probably averaging at about 3 years; though queens 5 years old and more have been known. A colony may rear queens for one of three reasons: either for colony reproduction (swarming), or because its queen is becoming old (*supersedure*), or because its queen has been accidentally killed or injured (*emergency*).

(a) QUEEN CELLS

A queen is reared in a cell which is quite different from the hexagonal cells of the workers and drones. When a colony is preparing to swarm, the workers construct *queen cells* in recesses in the brood-comb. Initially these are similar in size and shape to an acorn-cup, with the open mouth facing downwards. Into each of these cups the queen lays an egg. Like the worker-egg, the queen-egg hatches after 3 days and the rate of growth in the larval stage is even greater. As the larva grows, the queen cell is extended downwards. During these 5 days the queen larva is fed liberally, being virtually mass provisioned. Brood-food from the hypopharyngeal glands of many nurse-bees is poured into the queen cell so that the royal larva is literally floating in a pool of *royal jelly*.

On the ninth day after the egg was laid, the cell will be over 3.5 centimetres long, hanging prominently from the face of the comb, and it is then sealed. So generous has the feeding been that a quantity of food remains and the larva continues to feed for the next few hours.

Plate 9 A sealed queen cell. The princess is nearly ready to emerge and the workers are teasing away the tip of the cell in preparation.

Then it stretches out along the axis of the cell, head downwards, and prepares for pupation. This process is much shorter than for the worker and takes only 7 days, so that the fully grown princess is ready to emerge from her cell in just 16 days. The workers near the queen-cell become very excited and help release the princess by tearing away some of the material of the capping. Maybe the princess has rivals within the colony, in which case a fight to the death between them will quickly ensue, maybe she is to head a cast, in which case she will leave as soon as her wings have dried sufficiently. Then within a day or two she will begin her play or *orientation* flights.

(b) MATING

By the time she is 5 days old she will be familiar with the neighbourhood of her home and will take much longer flights. Often she will be away for 20 minutes at a time. It is during these flights that mating with a drone may take place, always in flight, high above the ground. A queen may mate with 8 or 10 drones in the space of a few days. Thereafter she will not take flight again until she leaves with a swarm.

The semen she receives from the drones is stored within her abdomen. The supply of sperm it contains must last her for the rest of her life, to fertilize the half million or so eggs she will lay in that time. Once she has mated, she is fed liberally by the workers, not with nectar and pollen but with brood-food. This rich diet causes her ovaries to develop fully and within 2 or 3 days she can commence laying eggs. From now on her life is devoted to this function alone. Nurse-bees near to her feed her continuously and are able to regulate her rate of egg production by the amount of food they offer. Others groom her, licking queen substance from her body and sharing it among the entire colony. If the supply of queen substance ceases, for example if the queen dies or if the beekeeper removes her, the workers in the colony are soon aware of their loss. Panic ensues. They search the combs and surroundings carefully. If they find her they guide her home rejoicing, but if not they settle down after a few hours to the task of rearing a replacement.

(c) FEMALE BEES

Now the workers and queen have one important thing in common— they are both female. Whereas the worker has become specially adapted to the maintenance of the colony, the queen has become equally adapted to reproduction, and yet both can be produced from identical female eggs. This remarkable differentiation takes place during the brief 5 days of larval life. A beekeeper can, if he chooses, take a young larva from a worker cell, transfer it to a queen cell placed in a queenless colony, and obtain a perfect queen, provided the larva is less than 3 days old. It is thought that for the first 3 days all larvae are fed on the same rich diet of brood-food from nurse-bees whose hypopharyngeal glands are at their prime. Thereafter, worker larvae are weaned on to less rich brood-food. Certainly these are observed facts. What is not clear is whether the nurse-bees are able to supply hormones which determine the change, and there is still controversy as to whether the shape and position of the cell have any effect. So in just 2 days, the fourth and fifth, of larval life this transformation is brought about. A colony which has lost its queen can therefore produce a replacement provided it has worker larvae less than 3 days old. A few will be selected, their cells in the comb will be enlarged and their feeding routine changed. In due course one will emerge, destroy her rivals, mate and take her place as queen.

(d) SUPERSEDURE

Thus a colony can rear new queens for swarming or to replace one lost accidentally. It can also rear a queen to supersede one that is ageing or failing. An old queen is probably unable to satisfy the workers' need for queen substance. Two or three queen cells are constructed and the queen lays an egg in each. From these one princess is allowed to emerge. She will mate and return to the hive and commence egg-laying. Quite frequently beekeepers find the young queen and her mother laying together on the same comb. This is the only occasion on which 2 queens can co-exist peaceably in the colony. Supersedure always takes place late in summer, the old queen eventually dying during the winter or following spring.

(e) COLONY COHESION

Although the queen has no governing role, her presence and well-being have a very profound effect upon the workers and they are constantly kept aware of her through an important piece of behaviour—*food sharing*. When two workers in a colony meet they are quite likely to exchange food, one offering nectar, the other

Plate 10 Worker-bees exchanging food. The one at the top is offering food to the lower one, who has her proboscis outstretched.

drinking it. This process is going on continuously day and night. Every bee within the colony receives and gives at frequent intervals, so that, in effect, there is a common food supply. This has important implications for colony organization, for each bee will know the scent of the available forage and all bees will have the same smell. Minute traces of queen substance become mixed into this common food supply and its absence will be quickly detected. I never fail to be amazed that within 15 minutes of removing the queen, every member of the colony will react to her loss. A swarm also reacts to the loss of its queen, for it will not cluster long without her but return home. These are the important discoveries about colony cohesion, the principles which enable the colony to behave as though it had one common mind. O. W. Park, an American, first reported food-sharing in 1923, and in 1952 it was confirmed by H. L. Nixon and C. R. Ribbands in England, using radio-active tracers. Queen substance was discovered by the British scientist Dr. Colin Butler, also in 1952.

The drone

Drones are reared in hexagonal cells which are slightly larger and longer than worker cells. Their course of development is considerably slower than that of the queen and slightly slower than the worker's. As you can see from Figure 7 in which the development of all 3 castes is set out, it takes 24 days from the laying of an egg to the emergence of an adult drone. Drones are normally fed by the workers on brood-food, although they can occasionally be observed helping themselves to nectar from open cells. Drones are larger than the workers, with a rather thick-set squarish appearance. They are powerful fliers, and though they make a very impressive buzz in the air they have no sting or means of defence. They do not leave the hive for several days after they have emerged from their cell, and they begin orientation flights when they are approaching sexual maturity, at about 14 days old.

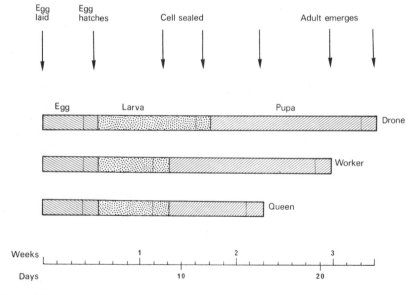

Fig. 7 This chart compares the development of the three castes during their juvenile stages.

(a) DRONE ASSEMBLY

We know little about the mating behaviour of bees except that mating always takes place in flight, high above the ground. Once it was supposed that the drones flew individually in search of a mate, but now it is known that they congregate together in groups. Queens on their mating flights appear to be attracted towards these groups, which may number 200 or 300 drones. Drones have powerful eyes and an acute sense of smell. Once an approaching queen has been spotted she is pursued by all the drones in the group until a successful mating has been accomplished. Each district has several drone-assembly sites to which some of the drones from colonies in the area make their way during their flights. Because of this, there is a good chance that a queen will mate with drones from another colony, ensuring cross fertilization. Drones take their flights on fine, warm days, most frequently in the early afternoon. A drone may be away from his colony for half an hour or more and apparently never alights during this time.

(b) MASSACRE

Drones are reared and retained in the colony only during the periods of the year when young queens might be produced: early summer, in the swarming period, until late summer, when supersedure is a possibility. At the end of the late summer honeyflow they are herded together in the outermost regions of the brood nest and soon after dragged to the entrance. In the struggle, their wings often get torn or bitten by the workers. Unable to fly or regain access to the nest, they quickly perish. The average duration of life for a drone is of the order of 5 or 6 weeks. In the harsh struggle for survival the colony cannot tolerate them during the winter months, for it has no need of them, and in spring it can rear more at will. Scientific research has not yet discovered in detail how this process comes about but the underlying biology is now well established and is one of the curiosities of the class of insects to which the honeybee belongs—the order known as Hymenoptera.

(C) PARTHENOGENESIS

Few animals are able to determine the sex of their offspring, yet
normally the eggs which the queen honeybee lays in worker cells
develop into workers (female), and those which she lays in drone cells
become drones (male). Just occasionally a very old queen may lay
eggs in worker cells which become drones, and a queen which is
prevented from mating also lays eggs which develop into drones.

A Polish beekeeper, Johann Dzieron, in 1845 put forward his
theory that drones were produced from unfertilized eggs, an effect
called parthenogenesis. This idea has been proved to be correct and
can be explained in terms of the number of *chromosomes* present in the
body cells which make up the insect. The chromosomes carry the
'blueprint' which determines every feature of the creature, including,
of course, its sex. In most animals and plants each cell contains paired
sets of chromosomes, one set from the mother (maternal) and one
from the father (paternal). When the reproductive cells (ovum and
sperm) are formed the chromosomes are reduced to a single set.
Fertilization results in recombination of a paired set, one maternal,
one paternal, so that the new individual will derive characteristics
from both parents. The sex of the individual will be determined by
the contribution of the sex chromosomes from each parent. These
chromosomes are denoted X and Y. Paired X–X they give rise to a
female, paired X–Y to a male. The ovum and the sperm, both
containing unpaired chromosomes, are said to be *haploid* whilst cells
containing paired chromosomes are *diploid*.

In Hymenoptera, the Y chromosome is absent. Chromosome
pairing X–X gives rise to a female (queen or worker) and unpaired X
to a male (drone). So the queen and workers are normal diploid
females and the drone an unusual haploid male. Queens and workers
therefore arise from the fertilization of an egg with a sperm, whereas a
drone is produced from an unfertilized egg. In the act of laying an egg
the queen is able to release some of the sperm stored in her
spermatheca in her abdomen. This would then result in the
production of another female. Whether she is able to withold sperm
when laying in a drone cell or whether the workers prevent

subsequent fertilization is one of the many mysteries science has yet to unfathom.

You will not now be surprised to learn that on the very rare occasions when a worker is able to lay an egg, this always develops into a drone.

3 · Bees and Plants

The relationship that has evolved between flowering plants and flying insects is one of Nature's most intricate feats. These two very dissimilar kinds of life have developed a mutual dependence to such a degree that neither could survive without the other. In this chapter and the next, I want to explore this relationship and examine the special organs that have been evolved to make it possible. We begin by reminding ourselves that the underlying purpose is the fertilization of the plant so that it may reproduce.

The flower

The plant's special organ for reproduction is the flower. There are many types of flower, each characteristic of a particular class of plant and each adapted to a particular means of fertilization. They vary in size from 30 centimetres or more in diameter in plants such as the sunflower (*Helianthus annus*) down to the minute individual flowers of plants like the grasses (*Gramineae sp.*) perhaps no more than 1 millimetre across. Plants may carry their flowers singly on stems or in various kinds of multiple groups. Sometimes these groups are so tightly packed together that at first sight they may appear to be one flower. The dandelion (*Taraxacum officinale*) and white clover (*Trifolium repens*) bear 'flowers'—strictly called inflorescences—of this type. Both are good 'bee-flowers'.

The important parts of a flower are shown in Figure 8. This depicts a very simple open type of flower, the buttercup (*Ranunculus sp.*).

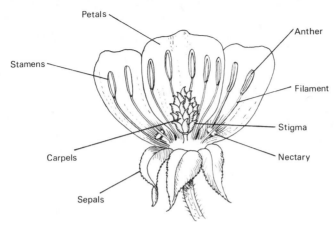

Fig. 8 Diagram of a typical flower, a buttercup
(*Ranunculus* sp.).

Find a buttercup, and with the aid of the diagram identify the parts
marked. Then find other kinds of flowers and try to identify the
named parts in those also. You will discover that the proportions and
prominence of the various parts vary considerably from species to
species. The most conspicuous parts of the buttercup are the bright
yellow *petals*, whereas in the marsh marigold (*Caltha palustris*),
which appears to be very similar, the petals are scarcely identifiable
and it is the *sepals* which are brightly coloured. The sepals form the
outer protective covering for the flower while it develops as a bud.
Together with the petals, they have evolved into a wide variety of
colours and shapes, their prime purpose being to attract attention to
the flower.

The essential parts of the flower are the female *ovaries* hidden
within the *carpels* and the male *pollen* carried by the *stamens*.
Fertilization is achieved when pollen becomes transferred to the
surface of the *stigma*, an extension of the carpels. The stigma may be
close to the carpel, as in the buttercup, or it may be held well above at
the end of a long *style*. The dust-like pollen is produced by the
anthers, which are at the upper end of the *filament* of the stamens. In
many flowers the carpels have coalesced, producing a single ovary,
style and stigma.

(a) FERTILIZATION

Plants have evolved many ingenious ways of bringing about fertilization. Quite frequently, this can occur with pollen from the same flower, though for reasons of heredity this is not desirable and many plants have mechanisms for ensuring that fertilization is effected with pollen from another plant of the same species. Many of the simplest plants like grasses are pollinated by the wind. The petals of such flowers are almost non-existent, allowing the anthers to stand clear of the flower. Their pollen is carried by the wind for considerable distances; much is lost altogether but some is eventually deposited on the stigma of another flower. It is these clouds of airborne pollen which cause the unpleasant symptoms of 'hay-fever' in many people. Some trees are also wind-pollinated. These usually have inflorescences of the 'catkin' type. Examples are the hazel (*Corylus avellana*) and silver birch (*Betula pendula*). The great majority of plants use the agency of flying insects to effect pollination, though birds, bats and rain are also employed by a few. It is, however, the insect-pollinated plants we are interested in here, and especially those making use of bees.

(b) INSECT POLLINATION

For what reason, then, should an insect choose to visit a flower? For the most part it is to obtain *nectar*. Hidden within most flowers, usually close to the carpels, are the *nectaries*. These secrete a sugary solution, nectar, offered by the flower as an inducement to its visitor. The nectar-drinking insects are equipped with long tongues and, attracted by the petals and sepals of the flower, use them to suck up the sweet liquid from the nectary. In so doing they inevitably become dusted with pollen as they brush against the anthers. The parts of the flower are so cunningly arranged that when the insect visits yet another blossom of the same species it is forced to deposit some of the pollen dust on to the stigma and so bring about fertilization.

Many insects fly at random from one species to another, so that fertilization is very much a matter of chance. To offset this some plants have evolved particular shapes so that only one type of insect will visit them. For example, the honeysuckle (*Lonicera periclymenum*) has developed a tube from its petals and sepals so that only exceptionally long-tongued insects will bother to visit it. Butterflies, moths and the larger bumblebees are the only ones able to reach the nectar. Other plants like the foxglove (*Digitalis purpurea*) are adapted to pollination by bumblebees and the garden antirrhinum has a flower which can only be opened by heavy insects and so is particularly well suited to the bumblebees.

(c) HONEYBEE POLLINATION

Bees of all kinds are exceptionally efficient as pollinators, for they visit flowers not only for nectar but deliberately for the pollen they also need. This they collect and carry away with them for use as a protein-rich food. A honeybee may have to visit as many as 500 flowers to obtain a single load, inevitably effecting cross-fertilization as she goes. Each pollen load weighs no more than 50 milligrammes at most and may be as little as 7 milligrammes in poor conditions. When we think of the amount of pollen needed by a colony in the course of a season, we realize the enormous effort that is required. It is not surprising, then, that we find the bees work to a very definite system, methodically covering a given area so long as the plants continue to yield. Each bee works within her own 'patch', often no more than 5 metres in diameter, for several days on end. She also remains faithful to a particular species, changing only when it can no longer provide her with the food she requires. This behaviour is known as *crop-constancy* and adds greatly to the honeybees' efficiency as a pollinator. When you have mastered the art of marking bees (see Chapter 5), mark some that are working in your garden, using a different colour for each one. Try to observe crop-constancy for yourself and get some idea of the 'patch' in which each bee is working.

As a further aid to reducing competition among plants for pollinating insects and ensuring selective fertilization, many individual species flower at specific seasons of the year, and even within that flowering period some plants offer their nectar 'bribe' only at certain times of the day. This can, however, give rise to problems when the farmer attempts to use bees to pollinate apples,

Plate 11 A Kent orchard at blossom time. Notice the strip treated with herbicide to reduce weed competition.

for example. We frequently find that the 'floor' of an orchard is covered with dandelions, which flower during the same period as the apple. Whereas the dandelion offers its nectar throughout the day, the apple does not secrete freely before mid-day. The bees therefore quickly locate the dandelions and work on them during the morning and, because they remain constant to this plant, often fail to work on the apple to any great extent. It is only by mowing the dandelions (in other words removing the competition) that the grower is able to secure the proper attention of the bees.

Pollen

Pollen is an interesting material in its own right. The individual grains have a tough outer coating with characteristic shapes. If you have access to a microscope it is possible to examine pollen grains taken from the anthers, though it is not easy to spread the grains individually. In size pollen grains range from about 5 micro-metres (forget-me-not, *Myosotis sylvatica*) to some 200 micro-metres (hairy willow herb, *Epilobium hirsutum*; hollyhock, *Althea rosea*). They vary considerably in shape, from perfectly round like mallow (*Malva sylvestris*), dumb-bell like forget-me-not and triangular like thrift (*Armeria maritima*) to Y-shaped like clarkia (*Clarkia elegans*). Many are beautifully patterned with nodules, spikes, whorls or mosaic

Table 1. Colour of pollen

COMMON NAME	LATIN NAME	FLOWERING SEASON	POLLEN COLOUR
Water Balsam	*Impatiens glandulifera*	Aug–Sept	off-white
Elm	*Ulmus procera*	Mar	grey
Mountain Ash	*Sorbus aucuparia*	Apr–May	grey/green
Meadowsweet	*Filipendula ulmaria*	June–Sept	apple-green
Rosebay Willowherb	*Chamaenerion angustifolium*	July–Aug	pale blue
Siberian Squill	*Scilla siberica*	Mar–Apr	deep blue
Willow	*Salix caprea*	Mar	yellow
Crocus	*Crocus aureus*	Mar	orange
Gorse	*Ulex europaeus*	Feb–May	chocolate
Horsechestnut	*Aesculus hippocastanum*	May–June	brick-red
Field Poppy	*Papaver rhoeas*	June–July	near-black

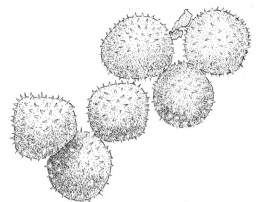

Fig. 9 Pollen grains from the garden crocus, greatly magnified.

textures. Virtually every conceivable shade of colour from off-white (water balsam, *Impatiens glandulifera*) to near-black (field poppy, *Papaver rhoeas*) can be found. I have listed a few in Table 1. When observing bees gathering pollen, try to note the colour of the loads and make up a chart of your own.

(a) FOOD VALUE

Inside the tough outer shell lies the living nucleus of the pollen grain. The digestive system of the bee is able to extract the nutrition from within. The food value of pollen varies widely and the bees do not necessarily prefer the most nutritious kind. Pollen represents the only source of protein which the bee has, as well as providing it with some fats, minerals and carbohydrate. Pollen from the peach (*Prunus persica*) contains a lot of protein, as much as 25 per cent, but very little fat. The dandelion, which the bees prefer, contains much less protein but up to 15 per cent fat. Some of the carbohydrate comes from starch-like materials in the grain but a lot is not genuinely due to the pollen, being from the nectar with which the pollen is moistened. Minerals account for about 3 per cent of the nutritional value, being chiefly potassium, phosphorous and calcium. As you may imagine, the number of pollen grains produced by a single anther is prodigious, particularly in the wind-pollinated grasses. It has been estimated that sweet corn (*Zea mais*), another wind-pollinated species, sheds as many as 20,000,000 pollen grains from each plant. Insect-pollinated plants appear to produce fewer grains than this, with estimates of 20,000 to 40,000 per flower for species of the lime trees (*Tilia sp.*).

Nectar

Nectar is the other important food which plants offer bees and which they collect avidly. Many other insects may sip nectar as their reward for visiting the flower and bringing about pollination, but again it is the special social economy of the honeybee which makes it the most useful insect from the plant's point of view.

In Table 2 I have listed the principal components to be found in nectar and tried to give some idea of how the amounts can vary.

Table 2. Composition of nectar

	% *by weight*
Water	30–90
Sucrose	5–70
Fructose	5–30
Glucose	5–30
Miscellaneous	up to 2

The miscellaneous component contains other sugars such as raffinose and maltose, dextrin, proteins, aromatic oils and acids. The 3 main sugars may all be present, or the nectar may be predominantly sucrose type, or contain fructose and glucose together. The total concentration of sugar may range from 5 to 70 per cent and this varies very much with prevailing conditions.

Bees collect nectar not only for their immediate use but in much larger quantities for processing into honey and subsequent storage. We know that the large colonies of the honeybee require vast supplies of carbohydrate food. Estimates vary, but it seems reasonable to suppose that an average colony in Britain may collect around 150 kilogrammes in the course of a year.

The amount of nectar secreted by a flower varies very much with different species, in some plants being continuously replenished (blackberry, *Rubus fruticosus*) whilst in others only slowly replaced if at all (ling heather). The factors which affect nectar secretion, both volume and concentration, are complex and far from understood. Nevertheless, we know that plants are affected by soil moisture, soil

Plate 12 The efforts of previous visitors to this blackberry spur (*Rubus fruticosus*) are clearly seen.

nutrients, soil acidity, temperature, humidity, sunlight and the time of day. Even the age of the plant or tree has an effect. A well-known beekeeper, H. J. Wadey, has recorded the case of a stand of lime trees growing in Sussex which, at the turn of the century, were renowned for their honey production. Now the bees scarcely visit them, preferring younger trees nearby. Similar cases are known for ling heather, blackberry and even clover.

(a) ENVIRONMENT AND TEMPERATURE

Some plants will not secrete if the soil acidity (pH) is not correct. White clover is a plant of the chalk downlands where the soil is decidedly alkaline, and the best yields from clover can only be obtained when it is growing on alkaline soils. Similarly, ling heather will secrete only on acid soils. In this case, though, acidity is not the only soil factor, for soil minerals and even correct altitude are equally important. The best secretion for many plants also depends on correct soil and air temperatures. Hawthorn (*Crataegus monogyna*) rarely secretes sufficiently freely to attract honeybees. It is only when the temperature is exceptionally high during its flowering period that they obtain anything worthwhile. White clover may not yield when the soil temperature is below 16°C nor when the air temperature rises above 25°C. Norway maple (*Acer campestris*) can yield freely at low temperatures (12°C), as can the wild cherry (*Prunus avium*).

(b) NECTAR LOAD

A bee may be able to fill herself to capacity on nectar from a single flower, but more often she will have to visit a large number of blossoms to complete her trip. Dr. C. R. Ribbands has reported observations of foragers working on *Limnanthes douglasii*, also known as the poached egg flower, a pretty little annual, popular with bees and easily grown in the garden. He found that bees needed to visit a minimum of 250 flowers for a full load, and in one case a forager took 106 minutes to visit 1,446 flowers before she was satisfied. Bees also seem to need to visit several hundred white clover flowers on each foraging trip. However, this may not be as arduous as it seems, for each clover inflorescence is made up of 60 or more individual flowers, of which 15 to 20 may be open at any one time. The situation is similar with other composite flowers like golden rod (*Solidago virga-aurea*).

Bees in agriculture

Many plants, then, depend on bees of all kinds for survival through pollination, while bees are entirely dependent even for day-to-day survival upon the plants. It is not until we remember that plants are necessary for our food that we, in turn, find we are utterly dependent upon their relationship with bees.

Try this simple experiment. Enclose a fruiting spur of an apple tree with a fine mesh netting (butter muslin or an old stocking will do) so that pollinating insects cannot enter. Do this while the flower buds are still closed. Remove the covering after the petals have fallen, marking the spur with a piece of coloured wire. Soon you will be able to observe that whereas small apples are beginning to develop elsewhere on the branch, they do not develop on the spur that you covered. Now, a few varieties of apples are able to set fruit from pollen from within the same flower, and if you happen to have chosen one of these varieties you may find small apples beginning to develop. If this happens, wait until the end of the summer, when you should find that the flowers which could not be cross-pollinated produce smaller and often mis-shapen apples when compared with properly insect-pollinated flowers. Lack of pollination, therefore, may not have such an obvious effect as is at first thought—it may result either in no crop at all or in a poor crop of low-quality fruit. Crops like strawberries which are self-fertile set fruit in the absence of pollinating insects, yet efficient cross-pollination by bees can result in a four-fold increase in the fruit produced.

(a) ANIMAL FARMING

At first sight one might suppose that there would be no connection between bees and animal husbandry. However, when we begin to realize that modern, intensive animal farming requires efficient use of plant products we find that bees play an important part here too. Cereal crops like wheat, barley and oats are grasses and wind-pollinated. Crops like oil-seed rape (*Brassica napus*) and field or tic beans (*Vicia alba*) are grown for the seeds they produce, which are rich in vegetable oil and protein. These form an important part of the diet of dairy cattle and intensively fattened beef animals and are insect-pollinated. Other plants such as mustard and lucerne or alfalfa (*Medicago sativa*) are frequently grown for animal food, particularly as silage. These are also insect-pollinated.

One other class of plants, the legumes, are of special value as a component in grasslands, for they possess root nodules which are able to 'fix' atmospheric nitrogen and make it available for plant roots. It appears that these nodules work best when the plant is setting seed—that is after it has been pollinated. Legumes include the clovers, beans and peas as well as vetch (*Vicia sativa*) and sainfoin (*Onobrychis viciifolia*).

Finally, there are the root crops grown extensively for animal fodder—all these too are insect-pollinated. Although most people assume that the value of the honeybee lies in its ability to collect honey we must admit that this really underestimates its true value to us. In fact, we depend on its services to the plant world for a great deal of what we eat.

4 · Tools for the Job

During the course of her life the worker-bee has to be able to perform many tasks. Over millions of years, nature has moulded and adapted the bees' ancestors, slowly evolving a creature fully capable of meeting the needs of its complex society with no other aid than those it carries on its body. In this respect it differs radically from that other social creature—man. For the majority of complicated jobs we have to do we need to be provided with tools. When a new situation arises we invent new tools to cope. The bee, on the other hand, is able to carry out only those tasks for which it has a specific tool, and when presented with a new situation it is unable to cope.

Learning ability

Whereas man has a large brain capable of original thought and of learning intricate detail, the bee's brain is very much smaller, fully occupied with its routine day-to-day behaviour and able to learn only a few necessary details. For example, music is quite inessential to our survival, yet we have the ability to learn extremely complicated sound patterns. Many other animals can be taught to perform tricks. The bee's learning, however, is restricted to remembering the location of its home, a pattern, colour or smell associated with a source of food, and the time of day at which food is available. Simple as these things are, they are nevertheless learnt with great accuracy and remembered for a long time. If a hive is moved a metre or two to a new site the flying bees will 'home' to the precise location they have previously learnt for the entrance. After a short search they eventually find its new position, but for the rest of their lives they will attempt to return to it by way of its original position. In other words, they have retained the position that the hive used to occupy in their memories and have added the necessary information to enable them to reach it from there.

(a) THE BRAIN

The bee's brain is, of course, in control of all her tools. It is not concentrated in one place like ours, yet it functions in a remarkably similar way. The bee's brain is divided into a main unit situated in the head between the eyes—the principal brain—and 7 *ganglia*, 2 in the thorax and 5 in the abdomen. Each ganglion controls the functions of parts of the body nearest to it, and they are connected together and to the brain by twin nerve fibres. Once the principal brain has decided, for example, to initiate flight, it signals to the ganglion in the thorax which controls the wing muscles. This ganglion then takes over, making the wings start to beat and controlling their beating until it receives a command to stop. This system avoids unnecessary signals passing direct from the muscles to the brain, as happens in mammals, and is very much faster in operation. Because of this the bee's reaction and movements are quicker than ours, serving the requirements of a flying insect particularly well. As might be expected, on account of the greater complexity of tasks, the brain of the worker is larger than those of the queen or drone. Even so, its capacity for original thought is virtually nil.

Food collection

A × 10 binocular microscope is ideal to study the external tools of the worker-bee. Maybe your school has one you can use: if not, a good hand lens will suffice. Capture a honeybee as she is working on a flower. If you make unhurried and deliberate movements she will not become alarmed as you approach and you are not likely to be stung. The simplest way to make your capture is to use a partially open matchbox and a piece of card. Having trapped the bee in the box,

Plate 13 A forager gathers both pollen and nectar from the flowers of the gooseberry (*Ribes uva-crispa*). Note the loaded corbicula and the position of the antennae.

slide it closed and place it in the freezing compartment of a refrigerator for an hour or so to kill the bee.

(a) POLLEN

The most conspicuous tools the bee possesses are the *corbiculae* or pollen baskets situated on the outside of the rear legs. The pollen baskets are vitally important, for they are used to transport pollen back to the nest. In the course of her visits to flowers the bee's body becomes dusted with pollen, either accidentally when she is foraging for nectar or deliberately if pollen is her prime need. You can watch a bee gathering pollen from an open type of flower such as the dandelion, or the Michaelmas daisy (*Aster sp.*), but you will need to observe very closely to see how she manages to transfer it to her corbiculae. This process usually takes place whilst she is hovering, though sometimes she will steady herself by hanging from a petal by one leg.

Pollen from the head parts and the thorax is gathered by the front legs and passed in a series of rapid, jerky movements to the *basitarsal brushes* on the inside of the rear legs. Pollen from the sides and underneath the abdomen is collected directly by these brushes. The *rastellum* (a series of strong spines) of one leg is then used to dislodge the pollen from the basitarsal brushes of the opposite leg, forcing it into the *pollen press* which is formed from the joint in the leg. By flexing this joint, the bee presses the pollen into pellets and forces it upwards into the corbicula, guided by the fringe of hairs. Within the corbicula, the pollen is retained as a compacted mass by the surrounding hairs. Some nectar or honey is always carried by bees collecting pollen, and this is regurgitated and used to dampen the pollen dust, thereby helping to consolidate the load. The bee packs

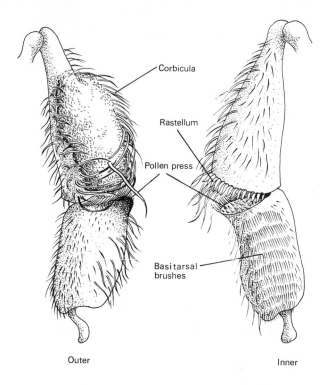

Fig. 10 Pollen-collecting tools on the rear legs of the worker-bee. The corbicula is shown partly loaded with pollen.

each corbicula alternately, little by little, so as to retain her balance in flight. Obtaining one pollen load may occupy the bee for 20 minutes or more.

Detach the rear legs of the dead bee and identify the parts marked in the diagram on page 67. Do this on specimens both with and without pollen loads.

Back in the hive, the pollen loads are removed from the corbiculae by spines on the middle legs. Locate these on your specimens. It is claimed that a colony may use as much as 60 kilogrammes of pollen in a season. A single bee can carry no more than 100 milligrammes at a time (probably less) so that this represents a minimum of 600,000 pollen-carrying trips.

Propolis is also carried in the corbiculae, but is roughly pelleted with the mouthparts and placed directly in position with the middle leg. Propolis carriers need assistance from another bee to enable them to unload.

(b) NECTAR

Of equal importance to the bee are her tools for collecting and carrying nectar. The long tongue or *proboscis* of the bee is an extremely complicated device. In essence it consists of three main portions, the central rod or *glossa*, and two pairs of membranes, the *galea* and the *labial palps*. These with their supports are hinged where the whole tool is attached to the underside of the head.

In use the labial palps and galea surround the glossa, forming a tube and leaving the end portion of the glossa exposed. The glossa is covered in hairs and when dipped in liquid can soak it up like a wick. As she drinks, the bee pumps the glossa in and out of the end of the drinking tube, bringing liquid with it. From here on the liquid can be sucked into the mouth cavity. You can observe the use of the proboscis under a low-power binocular microscope by capturing a live bee and offering her a solution of sugar to drink. The best way to go about this is to load a small paint brush with sugar solution and use this to 'bribe' a forager. With luck she will move her foothold to your brush and while she is still drinking you will be able to transfer her to a saucer containing some solution. When in use, the proboscis is held

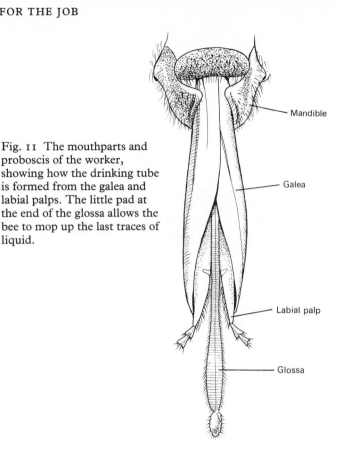

Fig. 11 The mouthparts and proboscis of the worker, showing how the drinking tube is formed from the galea and labial palps. The little pad at the end of the glossa allows the bee to mop up the last traces of liquid.

Mandible

Galea

Labial palp

Glossa

forward, supported by the *mandibles*. At other times it is folded back, tucked away under the bee's 'chin'.

(c) THE HONEY-SAC

Nectar passes from the mouth, along the *oesophagus* through the thorax. Entering the abdomen, the oesophagus leads into the *honey-sac* and it is here that liquids are carried. The honey-sac can expand considerably and when full occupies a large part of the front end of the abdomen, enabling a bee to carry very nearly her own weight of nectar. The contents of the honey-sac are normally prevented from

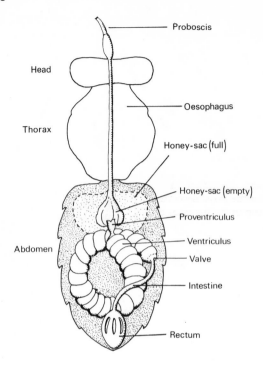

Fig. 12 Digestive system of the worker. When full the honey-sac can expand to occupy a large part of the front end of the abdomen.

entering the stomach or *ventriculus* by a special valve—*the proventriculus*—unless the bee needs food. The proventriculus is more than just a simple valve, for it possesses four folded 'lips' fringed with hairs which function to filter pollen grains from the nectar. When a forager returns to her hive, the contents of the honey-sac can be regurgitated into the mouth cavity and either deposited in the cells of the comb or offered to other bees (food sharing).

Digestion

The ventriculus is the part of the bee where digestion takes place. Enzymes released from the walls penetrate the husk of the pollen grains, releasing proteins within. A valve at the far end of the ventriculus regulates the passage of material into the intestine, where the food is absorbed into the colourless blood and hence circulated round the body. Finally the waste products enter the *rectum*.

Flight

We may, with some justification, call the thorax the 'engine-room' of the bee, for it is entirely concerned with movement. The plates of the exo-skeleton of the thorax are firmly joined together to form a strong shell with slight indentations through which the wings are attached. The bee possesses two pairs of wings and is mid-way in evolution between the primitive dragonflies (*Anax sp.*) and the true flies (*Diptera*). With the dragonflies, both pairs of wings are directly controlled by flight muscles and are quite independent. Diptera have evolved to a point where only one pair of wings is employed in flight, the hind pair having been reduced to hairs. The forewings of the bee are large and fully powered in flight but the hindwings are smaller and unpowered. So that there may be as large a wing area as possible, the hindwings are locked to the forewings in flight in what is one of

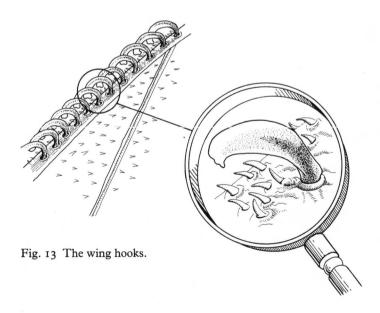

Fig. 13 The wing hooks.

Nature's most curious structures. Pointing upwards from the front edge of the hindwings is a row of some 40 hooks called *hamuli*. As the wings are brought forward for flight these enter into a fold on the underside of the forewings and grip firmly. The bee thereby has the advantage of the extra wing power while still being able to fold her wings neatly out of the way when working in the cells. Power for flight is provided by two pairs of massive muscles which practically fill the thorax. These do not act directly on the wing roots but cause the wings to beat indirectly by actually flexing the whole thorax. The hamuli are just visible under a × 10 microscope.

(a) FUEL

Before she sets out on a journey, the bee sips nectar from open cells, taking with her sufficient 'fuel' for the flight. The powerful flight muscles require large amounts of carbohydrate food when in action as well as a lot of oxygen with which to 'burn' it. For so small an insect the flight range of a bee is enormous, she is able to make a journey of 3 kilometres or more and return. Bees of a colony may therefore forage over an area of about 3000 hectares, which gives them a good chance of finding a continual supply of food.

Vision

How a bee locates her food is the subject of another chapter, but here we will take a look at the tools she uses—her antennae and her eyes. The bee has two kinds of eyes. Of the three little *ocelli* we know very little except that they are incapable of forming an image but are very sensitive to light. The 2 big *compound* eyes view the world in a way that is quite different from the way our eyes see it. In our eyes the transparent lens produces an image on the retina, a collection of thousands of sensitive nerve endings which pass the information to the brain. The shape of the lens can be adjusted by muscles so that the light rays are focused on the retina to produce an image of sharp detail. The iris controls the amount of light passed by the lens so that we may see well in conditions of widely varying intensity. Each

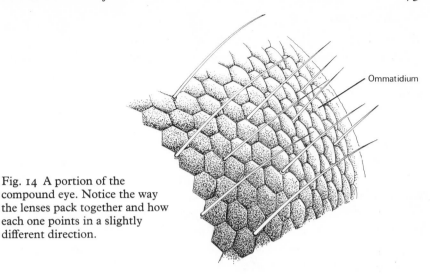

Ommatidium

Fig. 14 A portion of the
compound eye. Notice the way
the lenses pack together and how
each one points in a slightly
different direction.

compound eye of the worker-bee consists of a collection of some
6,000 simple eyes or *ommatidia*, each of about one-fifth of a
millimetre in diameter. The queen has fewer ommatidia than the
worker but the drone has very many more. The ommatidia are cone-
shaped in section and are packed closely together in an hexagonal
pattern. Each has a small lens which is incapable of being focused;
neither does it possess an iris. Light from the lens falls on a retina
consisting of just eight nerve cells. The image the bee perceives can
be hardly better than an impression of the brightness of the view
immediately in front of each ommatidium. However, the eyes are so
shaped that each ommatidium is looking at a slightly different point
within the field of view, producing a total impression on the brain of a
mosaic similar to a rather coarse half-tone newspaper illustration.
Although the bee cannot move her eyes she makes up for this by being
able to view a wide angle of her surroundings simultaneously. She
does not see fine detail, but her eyes serve her purpose quite
adequately, being able to distinguish certain patterns with ease,
particularly sensitive to sudden movement (and therefore danger),
and well suited to viewing moving images as she flies. In this her
vision is 10 times faster than man's.

(a) POLARIZED LIGHT

We shall see (p. 91) that the bee's perception of colour is totally
different from ours. Her vision also has a property which we do not
possess, namely the ability to detect the directional nature of
polarized light. Light is an electrical wave vibration travelling in
space. Natural sunlight, as it reaches the upper atmosphere, has every
possible direction of vibration in it. Wherever sunlight is reflected
from some surface such as a glass, or water (but not metal), vibrations
in one particular direction are reflected more strongly than any other.
The reflected light is then said to be polarized and the direction in
which it is polarized represents the *plane of polarization*. When we
view the blue sky we are looking at light which has been reflected
from water vapour and dust in the atmosphere and, though we cannot
discern it, partially polarized. Polarizing sunglasses are made up of a
material which permits light of only one plane of polarization to pass.
Now, when we look at the blue sky through them, the intensity of the
blue varies, being at its brightest in line with the sun and at its darkest
at right angles to the sun. It also varies as we rock our heads from side
to side. When the plane of polarization of the light corresponds with
the direction of polarization of the sunglasses the sky appears at its
brightest. Conversely, when it is at its darkest the plane of
polarization is at right angles to that of the sunglasses. This means
that if we can estimate the intensity of the blue light we can work out
the direction of the sun, even though it is hidden from view. It has
been proved that the bees are able to use the polarized component of
the light to determine the direction of the sun for navigational
purposes so long as they can see a small portion of the blue sky. In
fact, even light reaching the ground on completely cloudy days is
sufficiently polarized to enable the bees to navigate well enough. It is
believed that the eight cells of the retina of each ommatidium are
individually sensitive to a plane of polarization, so that the bee has,
super-imposed on the visual image before it, information about the
directional qualities of the light.

(a)

Plate 14 The bee's view of the world. In these photographs I have tried to simulate the impression of scene (a) as the bees would see it through their compound eyes. I took the photograph (b) through 8 segments of polarizing filter and printed it as a mosaic of approximately 6000 dots. Note the striking directional information the bee's brain receives.

(b)

Touch and smell

The bee's antennae are made up of two parts, the *scape*, a rigid, rod-like structure and the *flagellum*, a jointed flexible portion. These parts can be examined under a binocular microscope. The flagellum is made up of sensitive segments, 11 in the females, 12 in the drone, jointed together and to the scape which serves to carry the nerve fibres from the sense organs to the brain. The scape joins the face level with, and between, the lower parts of the compound eyes and

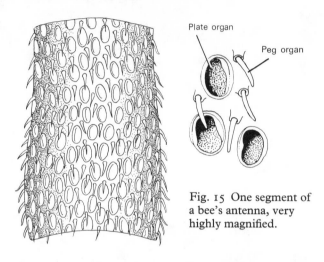

Plate organ

Peg organ

Fig. 15 One segment of a bee's antenna, very highly magnified.

serves to hold the flagellum well in front of the bee. Once again we have to admit that we do not yet understand fully how the antennae work and there is controversy over the exact functions they perform. Suffice it to say that they are as important to the bee as her eyes, for she spends a great deal of her life in complete darkness, finding her way about and performing her many house duties by smell and touch. We can demonstrate that both these functions belong to the antennae. When examined under a very powerful microscope, each segment of the flagellum is seen to carry two kinds of sense organ. Some, like conical hairs, protrude from little sockets—the *peg organs*; other are dish-like indentations often called *plate organs*. Set in the

TOOLS FOR THE JOB   77

antennae below each is a nerve ending which sends signals to the
brain. The peg organs are very sensitive to touch, while the plate
organs appear to be chemically sensitized, corresponding to our sense
of smell and possibly combining this with taste also. The number of
both kinds of sense organ increases considerably towards the tip, the
terminal segment being densely packed.

The bee examines every object she meets, either touching it with
her antennae or holding them close to it. We must conclude that she is
aware of the feel and the smell of objects around her. When bees
exchange food they continually touch their antennae together; just
why we do not know, but it seems likely they are able to gain some
information about each other in this way.

Anything that flies, be it bird, aeroplane or insect, needs to be able
to estimate its speed relative to the prevailing wind. We think that
bees use their antennae as 'wind speed indicators' probably making
use of the peg organs. Likewise it seems reasonable to suppose the
plate organs are able to detect water. The bee's sense of smell is very
acute and she can clearly detect the perfume of flowers from the
minute traces brought back on other foragers' bodies. At the same
time she can distinguish between many closely related odours in
much the same way as we can. The drone, in addition to having one
extra segment to the flagellum, has very many more plate organs. It is
thought that these give him an acute sense of smell with which to
locate a mate.

(a) ANTENNA CLEANER

The antennae are so vital to the bee that they need to be kept
constantly clean. For this purpose there is a special little tool in the
forelegs consisting of a notch lined with stiff hairs and a 'clasp' to hold
the antenna in place while it is being cleaned. The antenna is drawn
through frequently to wipe it free from all debris. This action is easily
observed though it takes place very rapidly.

Construction

(a) WAX GLANDS

The workers have two important tools for use in comb construction—the *wax glands* and the mandibles. The four pairs of
wax glands are hidden between the segments on the underside of the
abdomen. Comb-building bees consume large amounts of honey,
with which their bodies manufacture beeswax. Estimates of the
amount of honey needed to produce a gramme of wax range from 3 to
15 grammes. The amount probably varies with circumstances but

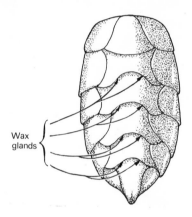

Fig. 16 The wax glands
are located between the
segments of the exo-
skeleton on the underside
of the worker's abdomen.

certainly wax is very costly in terms of honey. When secreting wax
the bees hang in loose 'curtains' from the highest point, often
remaining almost motionless for hours at a time. Their feet have
strong claws and they can support the weight of those below them
without effort, locked claw-to-claw with their companions. Slowly
scales of liquid wax are exuded from between the abdominal plates.
The scales quickly harden on exposure to air and are passed upwards
to the bees that are engaged in building.

(b) MANDIBLES

Using their mandibles, the builders knead and shape the wax,
carefully pressing each piece into place, fashioning the cells exactly to

the required size. Though they belong to the mouthparts the mandibles are nevertheless used more like hands. The mandibles of the queen and drone are not adapted for manipulating wax, being much smaller than those of the worker. It is often stated that the bees prefer to build their comb with the sides of the hexagonal cells vertical but I have frequently found comb with sloping sides.

Communication

There is another gland tucked away between the segments of the upper surface of the abdomen which is used as a tool for

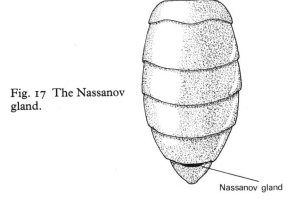

Fig. 17 The Nassanov gland.

Nassanov gland

communication. This is the *Nassanov gland* and it produces a pheromone which has a strong scent. This gland can be seen in operation whenever any form of disturbance has occurred and the flying bees are having difficulty in locating the entrance to their nest. The first bee to succeed, having alighted, stands with her head facing home and, exposing her Nassanov gland, fans the scent with her wings. Other lost bees quickly detect the pheromone and fly down the trail, each joining in to produce the scent as she reaches home. Bees may sometimes be observed using their Nassanov gland to attract others to a particularly exciting 'find' such as some spilt honey or an unusually rich food source. It is also claimed that the Nassanov pheromone is used by foragers to mark each flower as they work so as to avoid wasted effort.

Defence

Nature has equipped the worker-bee with an extremely effective weapon to protect her society—the sting. Hidden from view within a cavity at the tail end of the abdomen, the sting is a highly complicated tool and represents a very good example of the advantage of localized control by the nerve ganglion. Basically the sting consists of a *shaft* which penetrates the victim's skin, glands to produce *venom* together with their associated storage sacs, and the ganglion which controls the operation of the whole mechanism. The sting apparatus, complete with ganglion, can be torn from the bee in the act of stinging and continues to function independently of the brain. Though this causes fairly rapid death of that particular bee, seen from the point of view of the whole colony the system is outstandingly effective. Until the victim can remove the sting, it continues to pump venom into his flesh. What is more, in the act of removing the sting it is difficult to avoid squeezing the venom sac and so injecting the full dose.

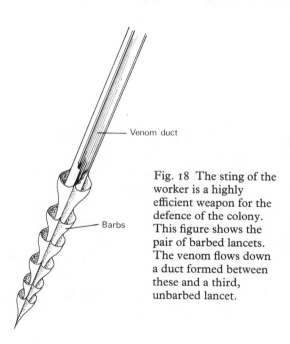

Venom duct

Barbs

Fig. 18 The sting of the worker is a highly efficient weapon for the defence of the colony. This figure shows the pair of barbed lancets. The venom flows down a duct formed between these and a third, unbarbed lancet.

The shaft of the worker's sting is made up of 3 straight *lancets* which are hard and sharply pointed. Two of the lancets have barbed ends so that once they have penetrated soft flesh they cannot be withdrawn. Powerful muscles and a system of levers act on the lancets alternately, driving them through their victim's skin; then venom is pumped down a channel formed between them.

(a) ALARM

The smell of the venom around the wound incites other bees to attack. When a colony is alarmed, some of the bees can be seen exposing their stings. At the same time they release an *alarm pheromone* which is quickly detected by the other bees and serves to put them on the alert. In the normal course of events bees will sting only in defence of their colony and will take no notice of us as they go about their work in the fields. You need have no fear as you watch them working in the flowers providing you do not molest them. It is very unwise, however, to approach their hive too closely, especially in their flight path.

(b) STING REACTION

In small mammals and other insects, the effect of a single sting causes instant death. In normal healthy human beings and larger mammals, a sting causes severe local pain which subsides after a few minutes, leaving a sore reddish ring round the point of entry. Over the next few hours the flesh in this region becomes hot and inflamed and often very swollen. This swelling may last for 2 or 3 days and is often accompanied by intense itching. The beekeeper, having been stung regularly over a long period, gradually becomes immune to the venom. I find I can receive 20 or 30 stings at a time (though this is rare!) without undue discomfort beyond the initial pain. A very few people are highly allergic and death from a single sting can sometimes happen.

(c) FIRST AID

If you are unfortunate enough to get stung, remove the sting as quickly as possible (remember it continues to work) by scraping it from the flesh and being careful not to squeeze it. Bathing in hot water assists the body to dissipate the poison and anti-histamine cream helps to alleviate the irritation. Stings near the eye or in the mouth can be serious and should be treated as soon as possible by a doctor.

(d) BEE FIGHTS BEE

When one bee attacks another the barbs on the lancets do not usually engage and the bee is able to withdraw its sting. Though the queen has a sting, I have never known her to use it on human beings. Instead it seems to be reserved for those rare occasions when she is involved in an encounter with a rival. Unlike the worker the lancets of the queen are curved and barbless, the contestants aiming to thrust into the opponent's abdomen through the softer membrane between the segments.

5 · Finding the Way

An experiment

When I began to write this chapter, I performed a simple experiment which you can do for yourselves also. But before you do so, please read the notes I have written on page 110. This is what I did. I made a solution of sugar in water, (50 grammes in 50 ml.), then, using the technique described in Chapter 4, I recruited a foraging bee and persuaded her to drink from some of my solution in a watch-glass—a saucer will do equally well—set up on a little wall in the garden.

When she was drinking happily I marked her with a dab of paint on the back of her thorax so that I could identify her again. Marking bees requires a gentle, unhurried touch. Use a finely pointed paint brush and poster-colour paint. The water-colour type is preferable to the acrylic, which tends to peel off. Approach the bee from behind so that she does not see you and deposit a spot of colour on the top of the thorax, taking care to avoid getting any paint on her eyes or wing roots.

The first recruit I marked flew straight off shortly afterwards. As she had not bothered to perform any orientation flights as she left, it was clear she would not be able to return to the food; remember I was trying to break her crop-constancy to the plants she had been working.

My second attempt was more successful. When she had drunk her fill, this forager inspected the dish carefully before taking to the air; then she flew slowly in ever-widening arcs over and around the site and finally disappeared from my view. I waited patiently and was

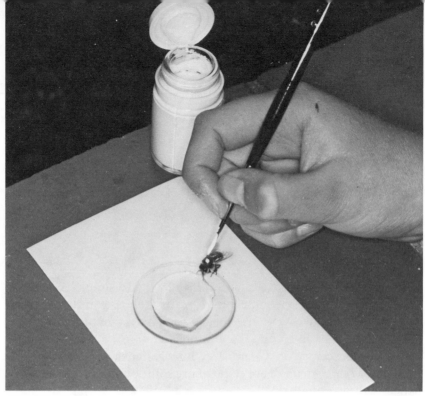

Plate 15 Marking a bee with water-colour paint.

rewarded some 20 minutes later by a return visit. She approached the dish with a little hesitation and was easily put off by my close presence, but soon she landed and began to drink. It took her about 2 minutes to fill up again and then she departed, more quickly than before but still making some orientation flight as she went. Half an hour later she returned again, then again and again.

Then something happened which was the object of my experiment. An unmarked bee appeared at the dish, soon to be joined by another. While the marked bee continued plying between the syrup and her hive, many unmarked bees began to appear. How did they find the dish? Did they come from one colony? Was it by chance, had the bees followed the first recruit or had they some means of communication? These are the questions that Professor Karl von Frisch set about answering as long ago as 1914 and which are still occupying scientists today. I do not have the space to describe von Frisch's experiments in

Plate 16 The feeding dish 2 hours after starting my experiment.

detail but what is set down here is a brief summary of the more significant findings that he and many other researchers have made.

Dances

Of course I knew some of the answers when I began my experiment. The bees were certainly all from the same colony; the chances of their finding my dish without some prior information would be slight. To begin with, von Frisch carried out experiments like the one I have described except that he set himself up a glass-sided observation hive and recruited his 'foraging' bees direct from this hive. He was then able to watch these bees on their return. He found that for the first 2 or 3 trips they behaved much like other foragers, handing over their load to the house-bees and hurrying off out again. However, once they had become convinced that their 'find' was both worthwhile and lasting they became more excited at each trip, and their agitated movements on the combs, as they handed over their booty, attracted the attention of other bees nearby. Von Frisch discerned a pattern in their movements and described it as 'dancing'. The bees that were close to the dancer were stimulated to go in search of food.

At first it was thought that the dances only served the purpose of arousing interest, but we know now that through them the dancer tells other bees in the colony where to find a source of food. After much patient observation, researchers have been able to unravel the code of the bees' language, for no description other than 'language' could possibly do it justice. I am convinced we still do not understand it fully, but the dances can be resolved into 2 distinct patterns.

(a) ROUND DANCE

When a scout-bee returns to the combs after locating a food source within 30 metres of the hive she partially unloads her honey-stomach before she proceeds to dance, pausing at intervals to offer some more of the food to potential recruits. The dance she performs consists of a series of rapid circular movements on the vertical face of the comb, reversing in direction every one or two turns. As she moves, the bee vibrates her abdomen from side to side. This dance appears to do no more than send bees out with a knowledge of the distance but not the direction of the food. If we interest a scout-bee in a food dish, say, 20 metres due south of her hive, bees will search for a similar supply all round the hive at roughly that distance; some will appear at dishes placed at any position roughly 20 metres from the hive.

(b) WAGTAIL DANCE

If a food source is located well away from the hive, 50 metres or more, the bees perform a different dance, called the *wagtail dance* by von Frisch [because during this dance the bee wags her 'tail' (actually the whole of her abdomen) from side to side]. This dance is much more subtle than the round dance for, by it, the scout informs recruits of the distance and direction of the food. The dancer moves in a figure-of-eight pattern with a 'long run' where the two loops meet. It is this run which appears to supply much of the information. At intervals the bee pauses to pass round samples of the food she has collected. In the darkness of the hive the bees use the vertical, in other words gravity, to represent the direction of the sun, so that a run directly up the comb would indicate the need to fly directly into the sun.

(c) DIRECTION

The angle the long run makes with the vertical tells the recruits the angle they will need to fly with the line of the sun. You will recall that bees are able to discern the position of the sun if they can see only a portion of the blue sky or even under complete cloud cover, by polarized light. If you have the opportunity of setting up an observation hive in your school you will be able to see these dances for yourself. One thing may puzzle you; in the light, bees give up using gravity as a direction marker and use the sun itself as a reference. It is amusing to set up feeding experiments and then illuminate the observation hive with light from the sky reflected by a mirror. The plane of polarization being reversed, the bees then fly off in the opposite direction!

(d) DISTANCE

During the long run, the scout vibrates her abdomen—the wagtail movements. The frequency and intensity of these vibrations give information about the distance and profitability of the source. The more rapid the tail-wagging, the more exciting is the find. Knowledge of the distance is important for the recruit for two reasons; firstly, distance coupled with direction obviously defines the position of the food and, secondly, the recruit needs to take with her sufficient food to 'fuel' her for the outward flight. It adds greatly to the efficiency of food-collection if a recruit does not take too much. Now it seems that the information the dancer provides is the effort it took her to fly home from the food. Since the recruit has to fly out in the opposite direction she will need to take account of the prevailing wind speed and direction, information which we believe is provided by her antennae.

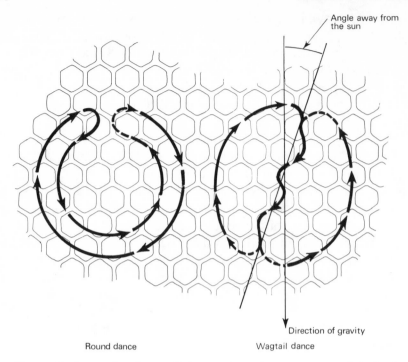

Fig. 19 Both round and wagtail dances are an important part of the bee's complex language.

(e) SOUND

Throughout the dance, the scout makes noises—short bursts of sound at a frequency of roughly 250 Hertz—just below middle C. It is thought she produces the sound by forcing air out through her abdominal spiracles. Between 10 and 30 of these tone-bursts are made each second, but we do not know their purpose. Some observers describe a third dance—the *sickle dance*—which is really a transitional stage between the round and wagtail dances. These dances are illustrated in figure 19.

Recruits

One striking feature of the behaviour of the bees that form the audience for the dancer is the use they make of their antennae. They hold them well forward, close to the dancer and frequently stroke her body, occasionally touching her antennae also. At frequent intervals the antennae are wiped clean by the cleaner on the forelegs. Presumably the bees' senses tire quickly, like our sense of smell, and this action refreshes the organs. In this behaviour lies yet another clue to the language of the bees—the scent of flowers.

(a) SCENT

We take it for granted that flowers are perfumed—most are vaguely pleasant to us and a few are highly odorous. To a pollinating insect, however, these perfumes represent a means of communication between the plant and the insect. The casual visitors, like moths and flies, are attracted towards the flower by the perfume that it offers. The honeysuckle is strongly scented only at night, to attract moth pollinators, whereas certain other plants, like some of the hellebores, produce smells like rotting meat, specifically to attract flies. Now, the hairy bodies of the foraging bees must absorb the perfume of the flower as they work and carry it back to the hive. It is this trace of scent that the recruits' antennae are able to detect, in just the same way as we can detect the smell of onions on our hands hours after peeling them. Hence the scent of the blossom now has a secondary purpose, enabling the recruit bees to associate a perfume with the distance and directional information provided by the dance.

We can demonstrate this in yet another experiment. Supposing we were to offer a scout-bee sugar syrup (which is almost odourless) scented with peppermint, and around the dish to which it has been trained we set out other dishes at, say, 1 metre radius. In some of these dishes we will place plain syrup, in others peppermint-scented syrup. The scout will continue to work the dish she has become accustomed to but the bees she recruits will find there are other dishes answering to the description given by the dancer and will visit any that have peppermint scents. Even if we remove the syrup and offer just peppermint they will alight. If we interchange unscented dishes with scented ones the bees will change position also, so as to remain faithful to peppermint.

(b) PERCEPTION OF SCENT

Scientists have been able to demonstrate that bees are acutely sensitive to certain scents, being anything from 10 times to 100 times more perceptive than humans. They are able to distinguish between some similar smells, like those of isobutyl benzoate and amyl salicylate, which we cannot distinguish, and also between meta-cresol and para-cresol, which we can. They can even be trained to associate smells of substances which are poisonous to them with food and to distinguish between mixtures of scents.

Appearance of flowers

So, when a recruit sets out, she goes with information about the quality of food, its flavour, its scent, the distance from the hive and the 'compass bearing'. The bulk of the journey she navigates by using her ability to perceive polarized light, but how does she proceed as she approaches her target? As she comes close to a flower she is aided by her memory of the scent, but what finally leads her to the nectary and its sweet reward? Do flowers look the same to the bee as they do to us?

(a) COLOUR

One of the great beauties of this world is the striking array of colour in flowers. Von Frisch studied the response of bees to different-coloured cards, by getting them to make comparisons between these and grey cards of corresponding reflectivity. Because they were of the same brightness, the bees could distinguish between the pair of cards only if they could detect the colour. He found that bees were colour-sensitive but their perception of colour differed from our own. The spectrum we can see ranges from deep red to violet. The bees are unable to distinguish red from grey of the same reflectivity, but can readily detect from orange/yellow through yellow, green, blue/green, blue and violet and then onwards into the ultra-violet. These are wavelengths which are too short for our eyes to see but to which the bee has great sensitivity. The bee can also perceive white—a uniform

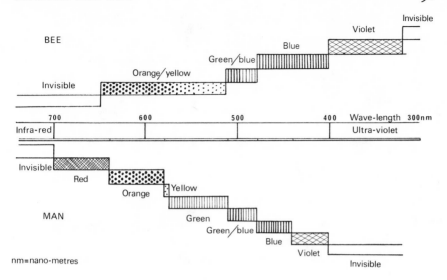

Fig. 20 Colour vision of the bee compared to man.

mixture of all visible wavelengths, except that bee-white would appear blue to us. Figure 20 is a chart setting out a comparison between bees' colour vision and our own.

(b) ULTRA-VIOLET

Bees, then, can see the colour of the flowers, but we must bear in mind that they do not see them in the same way as ourselves. They can use colour to distinguish one kind of flower from another. The fact that bees can see reflected ultra-violet light is also of great significance: two flowers apparently similar in shade to us may appear quite distinct to a bee, since the pigments of the flowers may reflect ultra-violet rays quite differently. For example, two white flowers, phlox and convolvulus, seem equally white to us but not to bees. Bees will work red poppies for pollen. They do not appear black to them; because they reflect ultra-violet light very strongly they must appear blue/green.

Plate 17 A geranium, left as it appears to us and, right, photographed by ultra-violet light. The prominent nectar-guides are clearly visible to the bees.

(c) NECTAR-GUIDES

One other feature of flowers is prominent. This is the *nectar-guide*— lines and patches of differing colour arranged so as to lead the insect from the point at which it alights on the petals or sepals to the nectaries. The routes the nectar-guides take lead the insect past the reproductive organs of the flower and therefore are also part of the flower's communication system with the insect. Nectar-guides are frequently scented, sometimes differently scented along their length, and in this way the insect follows a scent-trail as well as a visual one. The nectar-guides are not always visible to us, however, often appearing to be the same shade as the background, but they show up clearly in ultra-violet light. We have difficulty in distinguishing between three flowers of the mustard family, *Erysimum helveticum*, *Brassica napus* and *Sinapsis arvensis*, but to the bee there is no problem, for *Sinapsis arvensis* has prominent nectar-guides while *Brassica napus* reflects strongly in ultra-violet light. The red geranium in our gardens also has nectar-guides which are visible only in ultra-violet light, as you can see from plate 17.

(d) SHAPE

The shape of flowers is important also, for this provides an attraction not only for the routine forager but for the scout-bee also. Many classic experiments have been made to determine what shapes bees can see. Not surprisingly we find that they can distinguish between single lines and stars with 3, 4, 5 or more points, but these are typical flower shapes. They are not able to discriminate between shapes with unbroken outline unless the lengths of the outlines are different. That is, they cannot tell the difference between a circle, square or triangle, yet patterns formed from dots or lines (i.e. with well-broken outlines) can be associated by bees with food and they can learn and remember them. These would be features which would show up particularly well in the mosaic type of vision of the compound eyes. Many flowers which, to us, have unbroken outlines may well appear quite different in ultra-violet light on account of the distinctive shapes of the nectar-guides.

Within the colony, the advanced language of the bees, second only to man's, enables the colony to exploit its potential food supplies with remarkable efficiency. The 'language' which flowering plants have evolved to make best use of pollinating insects helps the scout-bees to find the flowers and the foragers to make use of them.

A new home

The scout-bees which are sent out by a swarm also communicate their choice of a suitable home by the dance language. The smell of the proposed residence must cling to their bodies and probably this also plays a part. Though the scouts investigate several potential sites, somehow or other the bees of the swarm make some kind of collective choice and finally heed only the dance message which directs them to it. Quite how this decision is made, and on what basis, we do not yet understand. The swarm does not always make the best choice as we would judge it, often accepting a home which will not afford them sufficient protection from the weather. They have a particular liking for taking over old combs left by a colony which has perished. As we shall see, this can lead to utter disaster.

6 · Honey

Man has been interested in honeybees for many thousands of years. The reason is not hard to discover. Our liking for sweet things was not easy to satisfy before cane sugar came into common use—a few ripe fruits and honey were all that was available. So strong was his desire for this delectable sweetmeat that primitive man was prepared to brave the fury of stinging bees to obtain pieces of honeycomb from the nests of wild bees. There is a fine cave painting near Valencia in Spain which depicts a man doing just this. This painting was made nearly 9,000 years ago, in about 7000 B.C. Throughout the ages since, honey has frequently been the symbol of luxury and prosperity, as, for example, in the Old Testament story of the Israelites searching for their promised land 'flowing with milk and honey'. In Greek mythology honey from Mount Hymettus was considered food fit for the gods and in England, until the last hundred years or so, practically every cottage garden had its hive of bees and these provided the sole source of sweetening for use in the household.

In our modern world honey is 'big business'. Canada, the U.S.A., Mexico, Brazil, Argentina, Australia and New Zealand, Italy, Poland, Russia and many other countries have considerable industries based on beekeeping and the prime reason is the production of honey. It is estimated that 400,000 tonnes of honey are produced each year, and consumption is rising steadily. Honey has become recognized as a valuable, wholesome food and is one of the few foods which is completely unadulterated during packing.

What is honey?

We have already seen that bees collect nectar from the flowers to provide themselves with carbohydrate (energy-giving) food which can be used immediately or converted into honey for some future use. What then is honey and how is it made from nectar?

Like nearly all products made from natural ingredients, honey varies within limits according to its source and the climate. An average composition is given in Table 3.

Table 3. Composition of honey

	% by weight
Water	20
Glucose	35
Fructose	40
Sucrose	2
Starches	1
Minerals	1
Miscellaneous	1
	100

(a) SUGARS

You can see that 75 per cent consists of two sugars, *glucose* and *fructose*. Glucose is the simple sugar which is present in our blood and is used by the body as a source of energy. Glucose passes very rapidly from our digestive system into the blood and it is this component of honey which makes it so valuable as 'instant energy'. Fructose is the sugar commonly present in fruits and has to be converted by the body into glucose before it can be digested. This process is a complicated piece of chemistry and takes a little time, so that this component is not available to the body until later and produces something of a sustaining effect. Honey is, of course, primarily a food for adult bees. It provides energy for muscular power and body warmth. Again it is the glucose component which is immediately available; fructose is temporarily stored by their bodies as *glycogen* and held ready for conversion to glucose as required.

(b) MINOR CONSTITUENTS

The miscellaneous component contains vitamins, enzymes, aromatic oils which are responsible for the aroma and flavour, proteins and amino acids. It must be remembered that these figures are average values and they may differ from sample to sample. For example, the water content of normal honeys may vary from about 18 per cent to 23 per cent while the sucrose content of clover honey may be as high as 6 per cent. Honey from ling heather is unusual in having a high protein content, which gives it the property of being a jelly. Even more remarkable, this jelly is *thixotropic*—that is to say, it behaves as a jelly until it is stirred, when it becomes liquefied. On being left to settle for a short while this liquid reverts to its original jelly-like nature. If you wish to experiment, non-drip paint is also thixotropic; stir some and observe its behaviour.

(c) GLUCOSE AND FRUCTOSE

Supposing we were to chemically analyse glucose and fructose. We would find that both contained the elements carbon, hydrogen and oxygen in the same amounts. A scientist would write their formula as $C_6H_{12}O_6$. Two substances having identical composition are called *isomers*. How then do they differ? The answer is to be found in the geometric arrangement of the atoms within each molecule. This variation causes the slight difference in the properties of the two sugars. It also gives rise to an interesting phenomenon known as *optical activity*. We have already encountered polarized light when we studied the vision of the honeybee (Chapter 4). If a beam of polarized light passes through a solution of glucose, its plane of polarization is rotated—the rotation being clockwise as seen from the direction of the beam. A fructose solution would cause a similar rotation but in an anticlockwise direction. Glucose is frequently known as *dextrose* (right-handed, clockwise), while fructose is known as *laevulose* (left-handed, anticlockwise) and you may find these alternative names in textbooks. Because they are both optically active and isomers, these two sugars are said to be *optical isomers*.

How do bees make honey?

Now glance back to Table 2 and look at the composition of nectar (p. 59). You will at once recognize the component parts of honey, but in different proportions. The variations are also much greater. In order that nectar may be preserved for storage it is necessary for the bees to reduce the water content from something like 80 per cent in nectar to the 20 per cent or so in honey. If they did not do this the natural yeasts which become mixed with the nectar during collection would begin to act upon the sugars, fermenting them into alcohol and carbon dioxide gas. Provided the water content has been reduced below about 23 per cent the concentration of sugars is too high for the yeasts to be active—most are not killed but remain dormant. If you take some honey and dilute it with water (to about 4 times its original volume) the resulting solution will start to ferment within a few hours in a warm room and you will be able to see bubbles of carbon dioxide rising to the surface.

(a) RIPENING NECTAR

The bees use two methods to concentrate nectar. A laden forager, returning from the fields, will regurgitate the nectar she has collected so that it forms a droplet between her mandibles and the top surface of her folded proboscis. A house-bee can now suck up all or part of the droplet and, seeking out a suitable cell in the wax comb, she will deposit the liquid as a droplet hanging from the roof of the cell. The natural forces of surface tension keep it in place. Often she will use a cell which contains an egg as a temporary store. During a heavy 'honeyflow' a beekeeper may accidentally dislodge these droplets as a sticky shower if he jars a comb! The natural warmth and airflow within the hive begin to evaporate water from the droplet. Frequently the bees add further loads of new nectar to these hanging drops. As the water evaporates so the concentration of sugar rises.

To assist this natural drying process one of the house-bees will come and suck up a portion of a droplet. Then in a quiet part of the comb she will slowly expel the liquid so that it is held in the fold of the proboscis just below the mouthparts. For this purpose the proboscis is moved slightly downwards from its rest position. Slowly unfolding and refolding her proboscis, she manipulates the liquid, causing further moisture to be lost by evaporation. After a few moments the bee withdraws the droplet back into her mouth and repeats the process over and over again. It has been estimated that it may take up to 72 hours to complete. Meanwhile the partially 'ripened' nectar is returned to the cells.

Plate 18 Bees ventilating at the hive entrance. The guard-bees can also be seen.

(b) SOME CALCULATIONS

When we consider that the final volume of honey is only about a quarter of the original volume of nectar brought into the hive and that a forager can carry no more than about 80 milligrammes at a trip, we come to the astonishing conclusion that it takes a minimum of 50,000 flights by the foragers to produce one kilogramme of honey. Now look again at Chapter 3 and note how many flowers need to be visited for each load of nectar. Let us now assume that each round journey covers 1.5 kilometres. We calculate that the total distance flown to produce each kilogramme of honey is roughly 75,000 kilometres or nearly twice the circumference of the Equator. Yet I have records of a large colony collecting 15 kilogrammes of nectar in a day in favourable conditions, although even half this amount represents a very good intake indeed.

(c) INVERSION

Reduction of water, however, is only half of the story of the transformation of nectar into honey. Look again at their relative compositions. You will observe that there is often a considerable amount of the sugar *sucrose* in nectar, which is present only at a low level in honey. Sucrose is the sugar found in sugar-cane and sugar-beet. You are familiar with it as the white crystalline substance you stir into your tea and coffee! The chemical formula for sucrose is $C_{12}H_{22}O_{11}$. During the processing of the nectar by the bees, sucrose becomes broken down into glucose and fructose. Sucrose is termed a *di-saccharide* because each molecule is compounded of one molecule each of the 2 simple sugars or *mono-saccharides*, glucose and fructose. One molecule of water is lost during the process of combination and this has to be replaced from the water in which it is dissolved when the di-saccharide is split into its two component mono-saccharides. This process is called *hydrolysis*—splitting by water. The agent which brings about hydrolysis is the enzyme 'invertase'. We do not know exactly how invertase is added to the nectar, but it seems most likely that it enters the salivary system of the bee from the hypopharyngeal gland and becomes mixed with the nectar whilst it is being processed.

A solution of sucrose is dextro-rotatory, whereas a mixture of mono-saccharides produced from it by invertase is laevo-rotatory (see p. 96). In other words, the direction of rotation has changed. This effect is called *inversion*, and an equal mixture of glucose and fructose, *invert sugar*. So now we can depict this part of the process in the form of a chemical equation

$$C_{12}H_{22}O_{11} + H_2O = C_6H_{12}O_6 + C_6H_{12}O_6$$

Sucrose   water   glucose   fructose

(d) STORAGE

By the time the water content has been reduced sufficiently and inversion completed the watery nectar of the flowers has been completely transformed into viscous, sticky honey. Now, ripened honey is *hydroscopic*—that is to say it has the property of attracting moisture from the atmosphere. Unless honey is kept out of contact with moist air it will continually attract water until it has become dilute enough again for the dormant yeasts to start their work of fermentation, and so it becomes spoiled. As the cells in the honeycomb are filled with ripened honey, the bees cap them with a seal of beeswax which prevents the entry of atmospheric moisture. Protected in this way the honey will keep for a very long time and is available to the bees whenever they need it, perhaps in the depths of

Plate 19 Sealed and partially ripened honey. Some cells are in the process of being capped with wax.

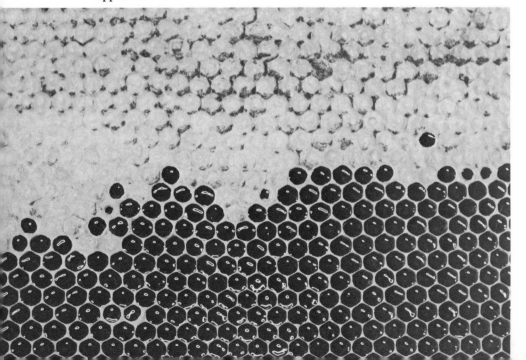

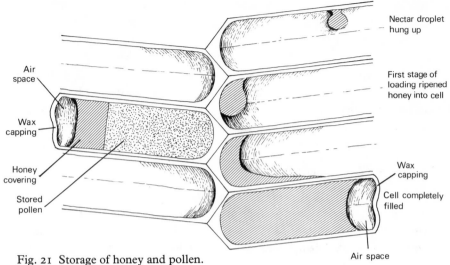

Nectar droplet
hung up

First stage of
loading ripened
honey into cell

Air
space

Wax
capping

Honey
covering

Stored
pollen

Wax
capping

Cell completely
filled

Air space

Fig. 21 Storage of honey and pollen.

winter. In a later chapter I will explain how honey is removed from
the combs for our use.

Crystallization

As it is prepared by the bees, honey is a clear liquid. Probably you will
have noticed, however, that a jar of clear honey left on the larder shelf
gradually becomes cloudy, thickening with time until eventually it
becomes solid. Sometimes this happens within a week or two, more
usually over a period of several months. Many people think that the
honey has 'gone off' in some way or 'gone to sugar'. The honey most
definitely has not deteriorated. What has happened is that it has
crystallized or, as most beekeepers would say, 'granulated'.

(a) AN EXPERIMENT

Try dissolving some salt (sodium chloride) in water. You will find
that you can go on adding salt to give a clear solution until you reach a
certain amount, above which some solid will always remain
undissolved. At this stage the solution is said to be *saturated* and if

you care to measure the amount of salt you will find there are 36 grammes dissolved in every 100 milli-litres (100 ml.) of water at room temperature. If now you try with some of the constituent sugars of honey, you will find that a saturated solution of glucose contains nearly 100 grammes in every 100 ml. of water (approximately a 50 per cent solution), at a temperature of 25°C. The value depends markedly on temperature, falling, for example, to 45 per cent at 17°C. Fructose is a little more soluble than glucose, whilst sucrose is considerably more soluble; a saturated solution at 25°C contains 68 per cent sugar.

(b) SUPERSATURATION

Now glance again at Table 3. You will be surprised to find that apparently glucose and fructose are present in an amount greater than for a saturated solution. This effect is known as *supersaturation*. Supersaturated solutions are not very common with inorganic salts like sodium chloride or copper sulphate but are found quite frequently in naturally occurring biological materials like sugars, where the viscous nature of these solutions helps to maintain this unstable condition. Supersaturation is, however, only a temporary state—sooner or later the solution must return to its normal stable state of saturation. In doing so excess material is thrown out of the solution as finely divided crystals. Now you can see that all honeys must eventually crystallize. They do vary considerably in the time they take. Honey from oil-seed rape and other plants of the cabbage family such as mustard and charlock (*Sinapsis arvensis*) frequently crystallize within a few days of collection: others, such as that from the lime trees, usually take several months, and honey from acacia (*Robinia pseudo-acacia*) may take years. Always they can be reliquefied by heating, though honey should never be heated above 40°C or its flavour will deteriorate and its enzymes be partially destroyed. Usually a small speck of dust, some pollen grains or a few microscopic sugar crystals will act as a trigger to set off crystal formation. The rate at which crystallization occurs determines the number of crystals forming and hence their size, fast crystallization producing many small crystals, slow crystallization fewer large ones. Because glucose is less soluble than fructose it is always glucose crystals which form first. The largest crystals found in honey can be nearly a millimetre long and produce an unpleasant, gritty texture. For this reason, beekeepers frequently add a small amount of crystallized honey of the right texture to a batch of liquid honey in order to induce rapid crystallization. The final product will then have the same texture as the added 'seed' honey. Properly crystallized honey should be firm but not so hard that you bend your spoon in it!

Colour and flavour

If you have the opportunity, visit the 'bee tent' at your county agricultural show or the annual show of your local beekeepers' association (or better still, the National Honey Show in London). Failing this, look along the shelves of honey at one of the larger health food shops. Take note of the range of colours which you see, from the palest straw yellow to the deepest, almost opaque, amber. You will find all shades of yellows and browns with hints of red and even green. If you are fortunate enough to be able to taste some of these honeys you will discover subtle variations of flavour, almost akin to wines. You may also observe that colour and flavour are often linked; pale honey usually has a mild flavour, dark honey a much more pronounced one.

In the British Isles, owing to our mixed agriculture, we seldom harvest honey from a single crop. More often than not ours are natural blends made from many flower sources. There are a few crops which grow in areas large enough for the bees to obtain virtually pure samples of their nectar. On p. 105 I list a few of these which you may be able to find, together with a few foreign honeys which I think demonstrate the wide range of texture, flavour and colour. Of course, there are many, many more. Look out for them and try them if you can; it is only in this way that you will find your favourite. It is interesting to reflect that this range is due to small variations in that 'miscellaneous' fraction in Table 3 accounting for less than 1 per cent of the honey.

I have devoted a full chapter to honey because the uniqueness of the honeybee depends so much on its ability to preserve its food, and also because it is this selfsame sweetmeat which first created man's interest in bees way back in the dimness of time and has maintained it ever since. I will add a short note about a variant of honey which you may come across.

Honeydew

Honeydew, in many respects, looks and tastes just like honey. However, its source is not the nectaries of flowers but the sap of plants and particularly trees. Anyone who has any interest in gardening knows full well that some plants are very liable to be attacked by *aphids*. These are greenfly and blackfly and a few other related species. Aphids attack soft parts of the stems of plants, usually close to the growing tips. Their mouthparts are capable of boring into the stems to extract sap for food. Now sap contains a lot of minerals, amino acids and also sugars. The aphids utilize the minerals and amino acids for their food, together with some of the sugar. What they do not use is exuded as a sticky liquid which bees find and collect. It is transported back to the hive and processed just like nectar.

Because the exuded sap is exposed to the atmosphere it rapidly dries, so its sugar concentration is often very high and therefore very attractive to the bees, who find it easier to collect than nectar from flowers on the same plant. Being exposed, the sap is liable to become infected with wild yeasts and fungus moulds. These become mixed with the sap and incorporated into the finished product, which is called honeydew to distinguish it from honey. These moulds often give the honeydew a dark colour, sometimes very dark, and they together with the amino acids and minerals from the original sap often impart a distinct 'tang' to the flavour. Honeydew from pine forests is considered especially fine in flavour.

Honeydew contains less invert sugar than honey but more sucrose, starches and minerals. It can best be distinguished from honey by examining it under a microscope, when irregular-shaped particles of the yeasts can be observed. Honeydew is also dextro-rotatory whereas floral honey is laevo-rotatory.

Some interesting honeys

(a) BRITISH HONEYS

(1) LING HEATHER—perhaps the most distinctive of all honeys. It is a deep reddish-amber gel which retains the air bubbles introduced during extraction. It has a pronounced, somewhat pungent, flavour, is much sought after and commands a high price.

(2) OIL-SEED RAPE—not very much liked by the beekeeper on account of its tendency to rapid crystallization, making extraction from the comb difficult. When obtainable in jars it is always crystallized and has a fine-grained lard-like texture, almost white and with an insipid flavour.

(3) LIME—also known as basswood. The lime trees are a common feature of our streets and parks and provide good honey crops for the beekeepers in towns and cities. The honey is variable in colour, from golden yellow to a dark greenish brown, and has a distinct, slightly minty, flavour. Left to crystallize naturally it usually sets with a somewhat gritty texture. The lime sometimes produces considerable amounts of honeydew.

(4) FIELD BEAN is a variety of the broad bean, flowers in July and is strongly scented. The honey is an attractive mid-amber and has a strong rich flavour. The amount grown has increased in recent years and is valuable as a source of good quality honey. It unfortunately suffers from the attack of blackfly (aphid) and is therefore heavily treated with insecticide, which has been the cause of considerable loss of bees.

(5) WHITE CLOVER is distributed throughout the dairy lands of the world. Probably 80 per cent of the world's honey comes from this source. In this country it is now much less frequently grown, owing to the changes in our pattern of agriculture. The honey is pale yellow, crystallizes to a fine, even grain and has a mild pleasant taste. It is probably this taste which comes to your mind when you think of honey.

Plate 20 The lime (*Tilia europaea*).

(b) FOREIGN HONEYS

(1) ORANGE BLOSSOM (*Citrus sp.*) from the U.S.A., Israel and Mexico. The name covers honeys from all citrus varieties such as orange, tangerine, grapefruit, etc. The honey is an attractive amber and has a pronounced flavour and aroma.

(2) LEATHERWOOD (*Dirca palustris*) from Tasmania produces a golden-yellow honey with an overpowering aroma and a strong but appetizing flavour. Usually crystallized.

(3) WILD THYME (*Thymus serpyllum*) from Greece and occasionally the U.S.A. This is a reddish and dense honey with a distinct and

pungent herbal flavour, truly earning its title 'the Food of the Gods'.

(4) ACACIA or LOCUST TREE (*Robinia pseudo-acacia*) from the U.S.A. and Eastern Europe produces a pale yellow and mildly flavoured honey.

(5) BUCKWHEAT (*Fagopyrum esculentum*) from the U.S.A. and Europe. It is extensively grown as a fodder crop and produces a dark brown, strongly flavoured honey which is usually considered an acquired taste.

7 · Enemies of the Bee

All creatures have their enemies, and the enemies of the honeybee include animal predators, virus and bacterial diseases, mites, lice and even moths.

Robber bees

Bees are not the peace-loving creatures we think them to be—far from it. Their society depends on their ability to acquire and keep safe a stock-pile of a highly desirable food. What easier way could there be to obtain honey than to steal it from another colony? So probably the greatest danger comes from other colonies nearby. We have already seen that every colony maintains constant guard at the entrance to its nest throughout flying periods. Any colony which is unable to defend its entrance, either because it is weak in numbers, or because it has chosen a home which is not easily defended, is in danger of being invaded. This danger is particularly great when there is a dearth of nectar-bearing plants, such as occurs in the autumn. At these times there is a large population of foragers who are unemployed. Once a scout-bee has located a weakly defended colony, these foragers can be quickly mobilized. If the attack is successful they can carry away large quantities of honey in an astonishingly short time, leaving their victims to starve.

Strange as it may seem, robbers often do as much harm to their own colony as they inflict on their victims. Sometimes even casual robbing can bring about utter disaster. The reason is that, as we shall see shortly, the 'killer' diseases can all spread through the agency of

Plate 21 A swarm entering a hive. The first bees to find their new home are using their Nassanov scent glands to direct the others.

honey. The good beekeeper is constantly on his guard to ensure that honey from any source is never exposed so that it attracts the attention of bees.

A warning

I have heard of many cases where well-intentioned people have placed empty honey containers outside so that the bees can lick them clean. You will now realize that, should the honey contain infectious spores, the bees that find it will transmit the infection to their colony. So safeguard the health of bees in your district by adopting a simple rule—*never* to allow bees to feed on honey from *any* source. Incidentally, these diseases have not the slightest effect on human beings and the honey is perfectly safe to eat.

Wasps

Wasps too are dangerous robbers in the autumn. They are stronger than bees and very agile fliers, easily out-manoeuvring the guard-bees, who rely on their numbers to repel an attacker. Fortunately, wasps do not possess the advanced communication system of the bee,

Plate 22 Guard-bees repel an intruding wasp.

Plate 23 The green woodpecker (*Picus viridis*) finds it easy to chip a hole through the wall of a hive.

so that each robber works as an individual, otherwise they would represent a major hazard. In some beekeeping countries the large number of wasps cause havoc at times among the colonies but in Britain the wasp is only occasionally a serious nuisance.

Animals

I suppose that traditionally bears are regarded as the prime enemy of the bees. This may have been so in bygone times, but nowadays bears have been hunted to the point of extinction, so that any damage they do must be very localized. In any case it is difficult to see how such an animal could pose too much of a threat to wild bees nesting high in trees. Skunks (*Mephitis mephitis*) are apparently a problem in some areas of the U.S.A., raiding hives to obtain honey. Like the bears they appear immune to stings. A much more serious threat comes from the smaller mammals, particularly mice, who raid the colonies after the bees have clustered for winter, building themselves a nest among the combs, which they devour, eating honey, pollen and wax, and no doubt benefiting from the bees' 'central heating' as well. Any beekeeper who does not fit a mouseguard to the entrance of his hives in autumn is likely to find he has been host to overwintering mice, much to the detriment of his bees. Some birds too have a liking for sweet things, while others are essentially insect-eaters and quickly learn of the increased activity in the vicinity of the hive entrance. The green woodpecker (*Picus viridis*) is well equipped to chip his way through the trunk of a hollow tree or the wall of a hive to steal the sweet comb, whilst tits, swallows and swifts can consume many a tasty morsel in the course of rearing their families. It is not unknown for toads, too, to sit patiently at the entrance, snapping up the occasional guard-bees who venture out to investigate.

Man

(a) PESTICIDES

It may seem strange that man could possibly still be an enemy of a creature which is so essential to him. But although modern beekeeping has largely removed the necessity to destroy nests to obtain honey, our very farming activities, which rely so heavily on effective pollination, pose a hazard to the bees. Many crops are treated at some stages of their growth with insecticides to protect them against damage by insect pests. Occasionally, through ignorance or force of circumstances, spraying is done while the crop is in flower and being visited by bees. When this happens whole colonies can perish very quickly. Unfortunately spray can also drift in the wind whilst it is being applied, falling on the hedgerows, weeds and other crops in the vicinity. Bees that may be working these contaminated blossoms are then at risk. There are even occasions when bees have to fly over a field which is being sprayed and in doing so are accidentally poisoned. All these dangers are considerably worse when sprays are applied from low-flying aircraft.

Many growers are well aware of these problems and are careful to choose the right time to apply pesticides, using materials known to have the least effect on beneficial insects. Some improvements have been made recently in the way these materials are applied. For example, the treatment of broad beans against blackfly is as effective when granular forms of insecticides are used instead of dust forms. The danger to pollinating insects is, however, very much less.

(b) ENVIRONMENT

The use of herbicides to control weeds both within a crop and around field boundaries can reduce the amount of available nectar and pollen to support bee colonies. The construction of houses and roads can have a similar effect, as can the clearance of scrub. Both honeybees and bumblebees rely on a steady income from wild flowers and trees to maintain their colonies between major honeyflows. If there is insufficient forage, colonies will die out.

The beekeeper has to regulate the number of his colonies within the limit his own district can support. The net effect is that there are often insufficient pollinating insects for the major crops. Growers then have to arrange for honeybee colonies to be moved temporarily into their area. Since 2 or 3 colonies per hectare are usually considered necessary for efficient pollination, the movement of a large number is sometimes involved for such crops as apples, pears, soft fruits, beans and rape in Britain, citrus fruits, buckwheat, and alfalfa in the U.S.A., and less common ones like onions (*Allium sp.*) and lavender (*Lavendula sp.*) in France.

Microbial diseases

(a) DISEASES OF THE LARVAE

Diseases are known for all stages of the bee's development with the exception of the egg. The larval stage is particularly vulnerable, for here the creature is exposed in a warm, moist environment in which one would expect micro-organisms to flourish. Many common yeasts and moulds do not seem to grow in brood-food, however, but it is not known whether this is because of some natural protection due to its composition or whether the bees add some kind of antibiotic to it from glandular secretions.

A bacterial disease called European Foul Brood (E.F.B.) is caused by a micro-organism—*streptococcus pluton*. This organism can survive for long periods in honey or on the combs yet remain completely inactive until it becomes mixed with the food supply of a young larva. Immediately it becomes active and multiplies, rapidly bringing about the death of the larva by about its fourth day. The dead larva decomposes rapidly, owing to the action of other bacteria. By their efforts to clean away the remains of the decomposing larva, the house-bees inadvertently mix some of the streptococcus with the food stores and so the cycle can be repeated. The beekeeper will observe the collapse and death of much of the unsealed brood of the affected colony, which is almost certain to die out eventually. Robber bees, stealing the unguarded remnants of the colony, cannot help carrying the disease back to their nests and in this way an outbreak can be spread rapidly throughout the district.

American Foul Brood (A.F.B.) is caused by the bacterium *bacillus larvae* and is the deadliest of the bee diseases. The bacterium in its resting form is highly resistant to heat and chemical antiseptics and has been known to survive for over 30 years in honey or on comb. Like E.F.B. the organism becomes incorporated into the food supply of the larva but it is not until the larva has been sealed into its cell, stretched out ready to pupate, that the disease strikes. Then, with incredible speed, the bacteria become active, multiplying many times over in a few hours, causing rapid death and decomposition of the propupa. As decomposition proceeds, the cell contents become completely fluid and then slowly dry down to a hard scale. The workers, sensing that something is wrong, often tear down the capping and attempt to remove what remains. In their efforts, of course, all they succeed in doing is further to contaminate the food chain. In any case, the scales become firmly attached to the cell walls and the bees find it completely impossible to remove them, so that henceforth the comb is permanently contaminated. As more and more of the sealed brood dies the colony is doomed to extinction. Again robber bees, finding the defunct nest, can hardly fail to carry the disease back to their own colony.

Both E.F.B. and A.F.B. are known in all countries in which honeybees are kept. Since these diseases can remain dormant on the combs for so long, attempts to cure them using antibiotics have not proved entirely reliable. The infection often reappears a year or two after the treatment. In many countries, therefore, infected colonies have, by law, to be destroyed. The combs are burnt and the hives thoroughly sterilized before being used again. The losses to beekeepers from these diseases can be so serious that in some countries periodic examinations of all beekeepers' colonies are made by official inspectors, as is the case in England and Wales.

(b) DISEASES OF THE ADULT

The imago (adult bee) also can suffer from several diseases, including some caused by viruses. Of these we know very little as yet, though they are the subject of much recent research. In Britain the most common of the adult diseases is caused by a protozoan *Nosema apis*. Nosema disease is widespread and, whilst not necessarily a killer, causes particular problems in late winter and spring. The protozoan is a single-celled creature and, when resting, forms a hard spore able to withstand dry conditions and resistant to temperatures of up to 70°C. Spores can remain dormant for 3 years or more in honey and on the comb. Once they have been swallowed by the bee and entered into the ventriculus they become reactivated and grow out a filament which pierces the cell walls and draws nourishment from their host. The protozoan multiplies rapidly within a few days, then, re-entering its spore state, passes from the bee with its excreta. By depriving the bee of some of its nourishment the infection has the effect of shortening its lifespan. If the bee is young it also reduces the activity of the hypopharyngeal glands, again by interfering with the digestive processes.

Additionally, the presence of the parasite causes the bee to become restless, particularly in the winter cluster. In normal circumstances bees void their excreta in flight, away from the hive. During prolonged periods of confinement in severe winter weather, their waste matter is stored within the abdomen in the rectum. If they become very agitated, the bees are liable to void in the hive, thereby soiling the combs. The effect of nosema is to bring about the kind of restless agitation that can cause this to happen. The house-bees in their comb-cleaning activities become infected with the spores. In this way, the disease can build up very rapidly in the early spring, at a time when the colony is in greatest need of its foraging force and its nurse-bees. As the spring advances the infection tends to subside, for the bees have a better chance of cleansing themselves away from the home. However, since the combs have probably been soiled, infection seldom disappears completely; usually it returns the following winter. Nosema does not often kill a colony directly. Its effect is more often to reduce the overall performance to such a point that the colony starves. As with the foul-brood diseases, robbing is the root cause by which nosema is spread from one colony to another.

Mites

(a) ACARINE DISEASE

In the early years of this century a disease epidemic swept through Britain, starting in the Isle of Wight and moving northwards, eventually reaching Scotland after about 10 years. By the close of the First World War, the worst effects were over, leaving the country virtually without any honeybee population. It seems that our native British bee had proved to be particularly vulnerable to the 'Isle of Wight' disease, and many bee-breeders are of the opinion that the Old English Black bee became extinct at that time. In the government-sponsored restocking programme which followed the epidemic, bees from several European countries, including France, Holland and Italy, were imported in large numbers. Many of the bees we have today are mongrels from the interbreeding of these importations.

At the time, the cause of the Isle of Wight disease was not known, but soon after a mite, *Acarapis woodi*, was discovered which appeared, at least in part, to be responsible. The disease was renamed 'Acarine'. The acarine mite is very small, being no longer than 100 micrometres, for it lives as a parasite within the first pair of breathing trachaea in the thorax of the adult bee. These trachaea supply oxygen to the brain and to the massive flight muscles. The female mites enter by way of the spiracles of a young bee. For some unknown reason they do not appear to be able to enter a bee more than 5 days old. Within the trachaea, the female lays her eggs. These hatch in a few days and feed as larvae by piercing the tube walls.

In cases of severe infestation, the flight muscles are seriously deprived of oxygen and become partially paralysed. The effect is to shorten the useful life of the foragers, thereby reducing the ability of the colony to gather food. In extreme cases the colony ultimately dies out. How the disease is spread from one colony to another is somewhat of a mystery. If they are in close proximity it is thought that young infested bees may enter the wrong hive when taking their play-flights. Drifting in this way is surprisingly common and, strangely, the very young bees are mostly accepted by the other colony. The mechanism by which acarine spreads over long distances remains unknown.

Acarine, as we know it today, does not appear to be as virulent as the old Isle of Wight disease and there is some evidence to suggest that the original ailment has either changed its nature or, more likely, was not solely due to acarine but was coupled with another malady. Nowadays we can cure acarine by using chemical vapours to prevent migration of the female acarapis from one bee to another or to kill the mites within the trachaea without harming the bees.

(b) BRAULA

Acarine is, of course, not strictly a disease, since it is caused by a parasitic mite and not by a germ. There is another strange creature which can live on the exo-skeleton of the bee. This is a wingless fly, a member of the order Diptera. *Braula coeca* seldom causes its hosts much trouble. The adults ride on the bees, spending most of their time in the joint formed by the head and thorax. They are very agile and can move freely over the thorax if disturbed. They feed by inserting their tongues into the mouth cavities of the bees as they are exchanging food. Many colonies remain completely free of braula and, of those that are infested, it is rare to find many workers carrying the pest. It would seem that any harm they do to the colony is confined to stealing a little food.

Braula has a particular liking for the queen, possibly on account of the large amounts of food she receives. Whilst 1 or 2 are the normal level of infestation of the workers, as many as 20 can be found on the queen. Here they may do more harm, by diverting much of her nourishment. The female braula lays her eggs on the cappings of sealed honeycomb and the larvae feed within this thin surface layer, boring tunnels along the cappings as they go. It is on account of this activity that beekeepers dislike the creature, for it spoils the appearance of honeycomb intended for sale. Braula can be removed from the queen with the aid of a little tobacco smoke, but there seems no reliable way for treating a whole colony. Within the colony the creature can easily climb from one bee to another, but it is not known how it migrates from one hive to another. There is, however, a very similar pest which lives on bumblebees—it may in fact be the same species. If you are sharp-eyed you may be able to see it riding on the thorax of queen bumblebees as they forage in the springtime.

Moths

The two species of wax moth are generally considered to be enemies of the bee. On the other hand, they can be looked upon as beneficial, for, by their feeding habits, they destroy abandoned comb and with it spores of foul brood and nosema diseases. In Britain the damage they do is largely confined to combs in empty hives or combs which the beekeeper has in store. In warmer climates, however, the female moths enter hives in large numbers, laying their eggs on the combs. The caterpillars grow rapidly, tunnelling through the combs and protecting themselves from the bees by spinning a silken web. Once they are in their tunnels the bees are quite unable to remove them. In a very short space of time the comb is reduced to a crumbling ruin.

The lesser wax moth (*Achroia grisella*) is a very drab little moth of about 1 centimetre wingspan and plain fawn in colour. Its larvae are about 2 centimetres long when fully grown, white in colour with a dark brown head. They pupate in crevices in the walls of the nest cavity, spinning themselves a very tough cocoon.

Much less common is the greater wax moth (*Galeria melonella*). This is altogether larger, having a wing span in excess of 4 centimetres. Still very plain, it is lighter in colour and its caterpillars have an orange head and one orange-coloured segment. Before pupating, the caterpillars excavate a hollow in wood in which to spin their cocoon. Neither species feeds on pure beeswax, always choosing

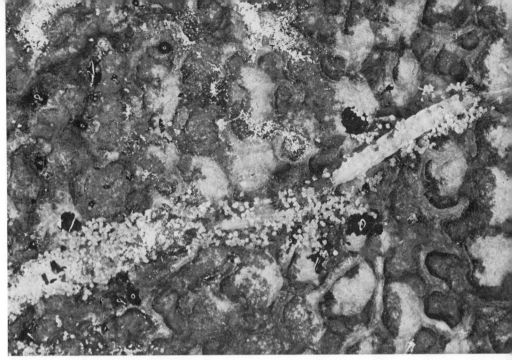

Plate 24 The larva of the Lesser Wax moth (*Achroia grisella*). Note the silken tunnel which protects it from the bees.

empty comb in which brood has been reared or pollen stored. They also appear to dislike honey.

In this chapter I have tried to give some indication of the diversity of the enemies that the bee is up against. Those described are among the commonest—there are others we know little about, particularly the virus diseases. In the course of evolution the honeybee has become what she is, partly as a result of her constant battle for survival against the combined effect of all her foes. In his beekeeping activities, man demands more from his colonies than just survival. For this he has to use his knowledge of the bees' enemies to safeguard his workforce.

8 · The Beehive

Hitherto I have used the term 'Beehive' to cover any domicile of the honeybee. In this chapter I shall use it in its proper sense, namely a man-made home for bees. Man's association with the honeybee goes back to the earliest of times and the bee is probably one of the first creatures which he attempted to keep for his own use. However, because of the rigid instinctive pattern of the bee's behaviour domesticated bees are really no more 'domesticated' today than those wild colonies that man first raided for honey. This regimen, around which the bees' lives revolve, places many constraints upon the design of an artificial home for them and on the system by which they can be managed successfully. Many fanciful designs have failed to become practical beehives because they have not taken full account of the instincts of the bee.

Logs and jars

In Neolithic times, man obtained honeycomb by raiding the natural nests of bees in hollow trees. He ate the comb, honey, wax and all, probably the larvae as well! He undoubtedly got well stung into the bargain. By early Biblical times attempts had been made to 'keep' bees and the first beehives had been constructed—simple hollow structures such as hollowed-out logs and earthenware jars. These simple hives are still in use today, earthenware hives being very popular in desert regions such as Egypt, Syria, Israel and Turkey, whilst log hives are more suited to less barren terrain, as in parts of Israel and in Europe, particularly Greece and Spain. By the time

Plate 25 Log hives are still in use in Spain today. (Photograph by F. W. Ochynski.)

these hives had come into use man had also discovered that smoke has a subduing effect on bees. By blowing a little smoke into the hives he could control and drive back the bees while he cut out the comb. Once the hive was set up and provided with a swarm as early in the season as possible, it needed no further attention while the bees built comb and stocked it with brood and honey. Then the beekeeper would rob the bees of as much of the honey stores as possible, leaving the bees with their brood to survive as best they could. I have no doubt that many colonies perished from starvation. This kind of beekeeping was only really suitable for the mild Mediterranean regions, with their short winters and prolific flora. Those colonies that did survive until the following spring would build up again, ultimately swarm and thus allow the beekeeper to make good his losses and increase his colonies.

Europe

The more severe winters of northern Europe meant a different approach to beekeeping. Here it was found preferable to destroy most of the colonies each autumn, removing all the honey and wax. A few colonies were left untouched to pass through the long winter, to multiply by swarming the following summer. The beekeeper wanted as many swarms and casts as he could get, each one being hived and allowed to build comb. Then in the autumn both the heaviest, that would provide a good yield of honey, and the lightest, that stood little chance of survival, would be destroyed. Those of moderate weight, capable of surviving the winter, were set aside to carry forward the stock for the future. The comb, when cut from the hive, would be mashed up and the honey strained from the wax. Wax, of course, was considered a very valuable product for making candles. It was for this reason that the monasteries were notable for their beekeeping, manufacturing candles for church use.

(a) MEAD

A by-product of honey-production and candle-making was the preparation of *mead*. In the process of washing the wax free from the last traces of honey, a liquor which could be fermented was obtained. Under the action of wild yeasts it would have produced a rather poor-quality drink, but by using the techniques of the winemakers a superb alcoholic beverage called 'mead' can be made.

(b) THE SKEP

Along with this thrifty approach to beekeeping went a more temporary kind of hive based on basket-weave or straw. Straw was particularly popular in Britain and the picturesque straw *skep* was a feature of cottage gardens until the early years of this century. It was both simple to work and cheap to make. The rural beekeeper was

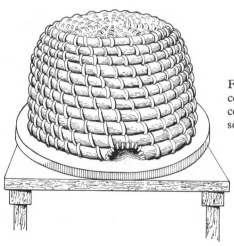

Fig. 22 A skep was once a common feature of English cottage gardens. It is now rarely seen.

completely self-sufficient and the system worked reasonably well, but there were drawbacks. Someone had to be around to capture the swarms and casts as they emerged; the colonies were often small because of natural division by swarming, so that honey yields were small; and it was not easily possible to inspect the combs. Added to this was the annual destruction of many colonies and the great difficulty of providing the colonies with any artificial food supply to tide them over difficult periods. An early swarm in a good season could probably yield 20 kilogrammes of honey and half a kilogramme of wax, but the overall average of honey taken was more likely to be about 7 kilogrammes.

Movable comb hives

Many attempts had been made to construct a practicable hive from which it was possible to remove the combs individually for inspection. The majority were unsuccessful because their designers failed to realize the fundamental principles by which bees build their combs, namely comb-spacing and the bee-space. Indeed, in the seventeenth, eighteenth and nineteenth centuries many of these 'hives' were laid out like human habitations! The great naturalist Huber and several others did produce a partially successful hive in which the combs were supported in wooden frames hinged together like the leaves of a book, but these hives were very cumbersome in use.

(a) THE BEE-SPACE

It was not until 1851 that an American, the Rev. L. L. Langstroth, realized the importance both of the bee-space and of the natural spacing between the combs. In his hive, Langstroth arranged for the combs to be supported within wooden *frames* which hung by lugs from rebates in the end walls of a rectangular box (see Fig. 23). The frames hang clear of the walls, floor and ceiling of the box with a gap of just a bee-space. He also arranged for them to hang parallel to each other, using the natural spacing of 3.5 to 3.8 centimetres, centre to centre. The bees respect these spacings, and although they coat the

woodwork with propolis they do not close these passageways, neither do they build comb in them. It is possible, therefore, to lift each comb individually from the hive without damage and without injury to the bees. Many millions of hives, similar to Langstroth's design, are currently in use throughout the world.

(b) FOUNDATION

In the first instance, beekeepers cut pieces of natural comb and fixed them into the frames, leaving the bees to make good any damage and complete the comb out to the woodwork. In 1857, Mehring in Germany invented a method of getting bees to build their comb directly into the frames. He found that if a colony was given a frame fitted with a sheet of beeswax which had been embossed with an hexagonal pattern of the correct size, the bees would use this as a *foundation* on which to build their comb. The bees cluster on the foundation, elaborating wax to lengthen the cells. Foundation is made in large quantities today and is often reinforced with strands of wire to make the combs less fragile. One of the advantages of the movable-frame hive is that if the top and bottom boards of the box are made detachable, it is possible to expand the hive by adding similar boxes to it, provided all movable components are separated by an exact bee-space.

Nowadays beekeepers have learnt how to inspect their colonies and detect the onset of the swarming urge. Prolific strains of bees have

Plate 27 A frame fitted with foundation. The reinforcing wires can be seen. The thickened portions of the side bars serve to space the frames.

been bred which enable large colonies to be maintained and with skilled management very large quantities of honey may be obtained. Yields of 300 kilogrammes have been reported in favourable climates. Here in Britain we consider 50 kilogrammes to be a very good crop whilst, with our fickle climate, our average is about 11 kilogrammes per year. Artificial feeding with sugar solution is easily possible, so the beekeeper can make up for any shortage of winter stores.

Components of the modern hive

There are many patterns of modern hive currently in use, but they are all based on Langstroth's principles, varying chiefly in the size of the frame that is used. The modern hive is essentially a stack of rectangular *chambers*, open top and bottom, in which the frames hang. An entrance for the bees is provided in the *floorboard*, and a *crown-board* covers the top. Over all is placed a *roof* to keep rain out. Hives are usually constructed in wood but experiments with plastics are being made, although the bees do not altogether seem to like these materials.

The lowest chambers of the hive are usually reserved for the bees'

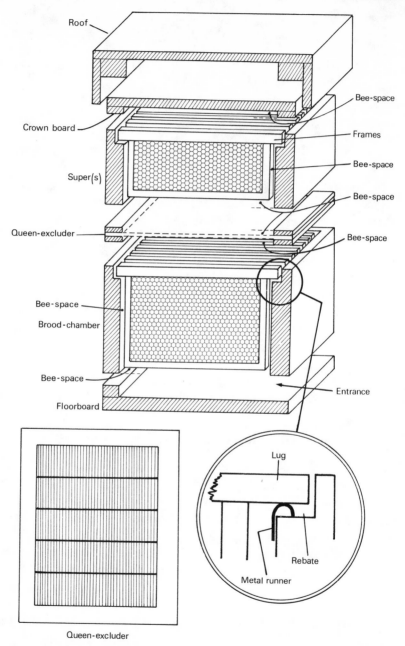

Roof

Crown board

Super(s)

Queen-excluder

Bee-space

Brood-chamber

Bee-space

Floorboard

Bee-space

Frames

Bee-space

Bee-space

Bee-space

Entrance

Lug

Rebate

Metal runner

Queen-excluder

Fig. 23 This cut-away diagram shows the construction of the modern hive.
Note how all the movable parts are separated by a bee-space.

permanent home. These are the *brood-chambers* where the queen is present and the brood reared. Above the brood-chambers are placed, in summer, the honey chambers or *supers*. Super frames are often shallower than brood-frames. Many beekeepers separate the supers from the brood-chambers with a *queen-excluder*, a grid of wires or series of slots which are accurately spaced so as to allow the workers to pass through but not the queen, who is marginally larger. The use of a queen-excluder prevents the colony from rearing brood in combs intended for honey production.

British hives

Although the Langstroth hive is widely used throughout the honey-producing countries, it is not very popular in Britain today, less than 5 per cent of our colonies being housed in this pattern. Instead the majority of our bees are kept in either the 'National'-type hive or the 'W.B.C.'.

(a) NATIONAL HIVE

The National hive is similar to the Langstroth except that the frames are smaller and it is square in cross-section, not rectangular. Each brood-chamber accommodates 11 frames, 35.5 centimetres by 21.5

Plate 28 The W.B.C. hive with the roof removed, showing the inner chambers

centimetres deep. A queen of a prolific strain of bees will need more comb space than this for her brood and often two brood chambers are used.

(b) W.B.C. HIVE

The W.B.C. hive is slightly smaller in capacity than the National, although the frames are the same size. The brood-chamber has space for 10 frames. It gets its name from the initials of its designer William Brouton Carr, a famous beekeeper at the turn of the century. The chambers of the hive proper are surrounded by an outer casework which makes this pattern very weatherproof, if somewhat more cumbersome in use. The shape of this hive is very pleasing and, neatly painted in white, it adds a most attractive feature to the garden.

(c) MIGRATORY BEEKEEPING

Because it has more parts, the W.B.C. is more expensive than the simpler single-walled hives, and it is not really suited to commercial beekeeping, nor to *migratory* beekeeping. In some parts of the world, notably Australia and the U.S.A., beekeepers move their colonies from one area to another to obtain a continuous succession of crops. In some instances the hives are permanently loaded on lorries or trailers, the bees being allowed to fly from each location while the crop lasts. When the crop declines, the lorries are driven at night to a new site. Provided this is done after all the bees have returned to their hives in the evening, none will be left behind. The colonies are always moved a minimum of 4 kilometres to ensure that none of the bees know the new terrain, otherwise they would attempt to return to their original site. In unfamiliar surroundings they perform orientation flights on leaving the hive for the first time and relearn its location. Migratory beekeeping is not carried out to any great extent in Britain, being confined to the movement of colonies to fruit orchards in spring for pollination and to the moors in the autumn for the heather.

The harvest

With the modern hive, there is no need to destroy the colony or the

Plate 29 A tangential honey extractor with some combs in the rotating cage.

combs to obtain the honey crop. Honey can be extracted from the sealed combs in a machine which functions like a spin-dryer. The *centrifugal extractor* was invented by Hruschka in 1865. The wax capping covering the honey is cut away and the combs placed in a rotating cage. The honey is spun out from the comb by centrifugal force. There are two basic patterns of honey extractor. In one, the combs are placed at a *tangent* to the circumference of the rotating cage and in the other they are placed *radially* around the central spindle. The tangential type is very efficient at removing the honey and only low speeds of rotation are needed. It suffers from the disadvantage that only one side (the outer) is extracted at a time and therefore it has to be stopped while combs are reversed to complete the job. The radial extractor is far less efficient, for it relies on the slight upward tilt the bees give to the cells of their combs to enable the honey to be thrown out. However, both sides of the combs are extracted simultaneously and a greater number of combs can be accommodated

Plate 30 A comb of sealed honey. This comb would contain nearly 1.5 kilogrammes.

in a given cage diameter. Much higher speeds are required and it may take 20 minutes or so to empty the combs completely, so that this pattern is really only suited to the large, power-driven machines used by commercial beekeepers. The amateur, with a few hives, usually uses a tangential extractor driven by hand.

Honey, as it comes from the extractor, contains air bubbles and particles of wax. The wax is usually removed by straining, the honey being left to stand for a while to allow the air bubbles to rise. Thereafter it is ready for packing. The extracted combs are virtually undamaged and may be returned to the bees and re-used repeatedly.

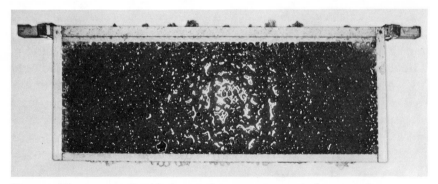

Plate 31 The same comb with the cappings cut away ready for extraction.

Plate 32 A young beekeeper inspects a colony in a National hive. Note her veil and smoker, and the hive-tool with which the frames are prised up.

Beekeeping

So the modern hive allows the beekeeper to inspect his colonies, to observe their development, expand their home and obtain his harvest without injury to the bees or damage to their combs. His greatest aid in controlling the bees is still smoke. When smoke is puffed into the hive it causes the bees to gorge on honey, and, for a reason we do not yet understand, they become less likely to sting. A beekeeper may wear a *veil* to keep the bees away from his face and particularly his eyes, and he may wear protective clothing and gloves. Handling a colony of bees so that there is the minimum risk of being stung is an art which requires not only practice and skill but also a keen understanding of the bee and its world.

9 · Finding Out More

This book will have provided the background to the natural history and behaviour of bees as well as supplying a little information about beekeeping. The world of the bee is so diverse, bordering as it does on the division between two major classes of living things, that each of us can choose our paths of further study. It may be social insects, plants and pollination, behaviour, learning ability, navigation or communication.

Throughout the world, scientists are active, patiently unravelling the bees' secrets, for much of their behaviour is also relevant to man. The books scientists write about their work are often highly technical and specialized, but many of the best of them are also excellent writers. In the list of books that follows (p. 136) I have included some scientific studies of bees and some practical works on beekeeping. Now go and find out more.

Observation hive

In a subject like this, there really is no substitute for first-hand observation. A glass-sided observation hive containing a miniature colony of bees can be highly instructive, for here you will be able to see, in action, much of what I have written about. Your County Beekeeping Instructor should be able to assist your school to get one set up. He is a busy person, so do not leave your request until late in the spring, or you may be disappointed. An alternative may be to seek the co-operation of your local beekeepers' association. Your local library should have a note of the secretary's name.

Plate 33 Interest at the observation hive.

Keeping bees

You may be tempted to try your hand at keeping bees. Properly undertaken it is an excellent hobby and of great value to the agriculture of the country. Let me warn you, however, that in unskilled hands a colony of bees can be a nuisance and a danger to yourself and your neighbours. Before you start, join your local beekeeping association. You will get to know others already in the craft and be able to see what it is all about before getting involved. Most associations have regular meetings when you can benefit from the knowledge of others and some provide organized courses of instruction for novices. The local secretary will be glad to help you. There are also evening classes in some areas and he will know about these as well.

One final little point. You may find beehives dotted about the countryside. By all means watch the activities of the bees, but do please remember that these are someone's property and do not attempt to take a peep inside. You may cause the beekeeper considerable disruption to his management, to say nothing of the risk of getting yourself stung.

Appendix

Further reading

(a) BOOKS OF GENERAL INTEREST

British Beekeepers Association, *Honeybee Anatomy*, B.B.K.A., Sevenoaks, 1977

Butler, C., *The World of the Honeybee*, Collins, London, 1974

Dalton, S., *Borne on the Wind: The Extraordinary World of Insects in Flight*, Chatto and Windus, London, 1975

Dines, A. M. and Dalton, S., *Honeybees from Close Up*, Cassell, London, 1968

Doering, H., *A Bee is Born*, Sterling, New York, 1973

d'Entreves, P. P. and Zunino, M., *The Secret Life of Insects*, Orbis, London, 1976

Farb, P., *The Insects*, Time, New York, 1962

Fraser, H. M., *Beekeeping in Antiquity*, University of London Press, 1951

Free, J. B. and Butler, C., *Bumblebees*, Collins, London, 1968

von Frisch, K., *The Dancing Bees*, Methuen, London, 1966

von Frisch, K., *The Foraging Bee. How she finds and exploits sources of food*, I.B.R.A., Chalfont St. Peter, Bucks., 1970

Hodges, D., *Pollen Loads of the Honeybee*, I.B.R.A., Chalfont St. Peter, Bucks., 1975

Martin, W. Keeble, *The Concise British Flora in Colour*, Ebury Press, London, 1959

More, D., *The Bee Book: The history and natural history of the honeybee*, David and Charles, Newton Abbot, 1976

(b) MORE ADVANCED BOOKS

Bailey, L., *Infectious Diseases of the Honeybee*, Land Books, London, 1963

Crane, E., *Honey: A Comprehensive Survey*, I.B.R.A., Chalfont, 1976

Dade, H. A., *Anatomy and Dissection of the Honeybee*, I.B.R.A., Chalfont St. Peter, Bucks., 1977

von Frisch, K., *The Dance Language and Orientation of Bees*, Oxford University Press, London, 1967

Ribbands, C. R., *The Behaviour and Social Life of Honeybees*, Dover Publications, New York, 1965

(c) INTRODUCTORY BOOKS ON BEEKEEPING

Couston, R., *Principles of Practical Beekeeping*, Geo. Outram, London, 1972

Hamilton, W., *The Art of Beekeeping*, The Herald Printers, York, 1971

Hooper, Ted, *Guide to Bees and Honey*, Blandford Press, Poole, 1976

Ministry of Agriculture, Fisheries and Food, Bulletin No. 100, *Diseases of Bees*, H.M.S.O., London, 1970

Ministry of Agriculture, Fisheries and Food, Bulletin No. 144, *Beehives*, H.M.S.O., London, 1968

Ministry of Agriculture, Fisheries and Food, Bulletin No. 206, *Swarming*, H.M.S.O., London, 1970

Pavord, A. V., *Bees and Beekeeping*, Cassell, London, 1975

Riches, H. R. C., *Beekeeping*, Foyles Handbooks, London, 1976

Stevens, K., *Apiculture in Schools*, British Bee Publications, Northants, 1977

Wall charts

Bees illustrates a solitary bee (*Adrena amata*), a social bee (*Bombus terrestris*) and the honeybee.

The Honeybee sets out the natural history of the honeybee in diagrammatic form.

Both are published by Educational Productions Ltd. in collaboration
with I.B.R.A., Chalfont St. Peter, Bucks.
Set of 12 Study Prints on the Honeybee, McGraw-Hill, U.S.A.
Available from I.B.R.A., Chalfont St. Peter, Bucks.

Useful addresses

British Beekeepers Association (B.B.K.A.), General Secretary, 55
Chipstead Lane, Sevenoaks, Kent, TN13 2AJ

Welsh Beekeepers Association, General Secretary, Tyn-y-Berllan,
Builth Wells

Scottish Beekeepers Association, General Secretary, 26 The
Meadows, Berwick-on-Tweed, Northumberland, TD15 1NY

International Bee Research Association (I.B.R.A.), Hill House,
Chalfont St Peter, Bucks, SL9 0NR

Central Association of Beekeepers, Hon. Secretary, Long Reach,
Stockbury Valley, Sittingbourne, Kent

National Beekeeping Advisers, Luddington Experimental Horticul-
tural Station, Stratford on Avon, Warwickshire

Index